The Happy Face Killer An Anthology of True Crime

Ruth Kanton

Published by Trellis Publishing, 2021.

While every precaution has been taken in the preparation of this book, the publisher assumes no responsibility for errors or omissions, or for damages resulting from the use of the information contained herein.

THE HAPPY FACE KILLER AN ANTHOLOGY OF TRUE CRIME

First edition. June 30, 2021.

Copyright © 2021 Ruth Kanton.

ISBN: 979-8224944903

Written by Ruth Kanton.

THE HAPPY FACE KILLER

RUTH KANTON

<u>THE HAPPY FACE KILLER</u>
<u>LAUREN STUART</u>
<u>ISRAEL KEYES</u>
<u>SISTER MARGARET PAHL</u>
<u>MICHELE AVILA</u>
<u>GEORGE BANKS</u>

Born on April 6, 1955, in Chilliwack, British Columbia, Canada, to Leslie and Gladys Jesperson, Keith Hunter Jesperson was the third of five children. His father Leslie was a domineering alcoholic prone to abusing his wife and children, but he vehemently denied these claims. However, a number of relatives later confirmed that he was indeed abusive, and he would go as far as punishing Jesperson by electric shock. Jesperson was physically large for his age, and this resulted in endless teasing by friends and family. He was treated as an outcast at home, with his brothers nicknaming him "Igor," which was often shortened to "Ig." The nickname stuck throughout his school years. Jesperson grew up as a lonely kid, always content to play on his own. He began getting into trouble often, which resulted in severe punishments from his father.

Jesperson also had a sadistic personality, and from a young age, he frequently tortured and killed animals. He enjoyed killing them, as well as watching the animals kill each other. This habit went on as he grew up, and he began wondering what it was like to kill a human being. When the family moved to a trailer park in Selah, Washington, Jesperson would capture stray cats, dogs, and birds, beat them severely before strangling them. On two occasions, Jesperson got into trouble for attempted murder. When he was 10 years old, Jesperson often got into trouble with another boy, Martin. However, Martin would often blame Jesperson for things he didn't do, which outraged Jesperson. This came to a head when Jesperson attacked Martin and beat him violently. He only stopped when his father intervened, later stating that he intended to kill the boy. About a year after this incident, he was swimming in a lake when he was held underwater by another boy until he passed out. Jesperson waited for the opportunity to exact revenge, which came sometime later at a public pool. Jesperson approached the boy and attempted to drown him by holding his head underwater. His plan was thwarted when the lifeguard intervened by pulling him away.

Jesperson graduated from high school in 1973, but made no plans to attend college because his father didn't believe he could make it. By 1974, Jesperson had been hired as a truck driver. In 1975, at age 20, he married Rose Hucke, whom he had been dating since he completed high school. The couple went on to have three children – two girls and a boy. However, a few years into the marriage, Hucke began receiving numerous calls from random women looking for her husband, leading her to suspect Jesperson was being unfaithful. As the years went by, problems in the marriage kept growing, and the couple split after 14 years. When Jesperson was out on the road, Hucke packed up and left with the children to live in Spokane, Washington, with her parents. Their divorce was finalized in 1990.

In the same year, 35-year-old Jesperson began training for his dream job – becoming a Royal Canadian Mounted Policeman. However, his plans were cut short when he suffered an injury, forcing him to seek work as a truck driver once again following his relocation to Cheney, Washington.

The Murder of Taunja Bennett

On January 23, 1990, a college student driving around in the outskirts of Portland, Oregon, noticed a body lying in an embankment off the highway. The young woman was half-naked, and investigators discovered that she had been strangled, the rope still looped tightly around her neck. She had been sexually assaulted and viciously beaten, her face taking the brunt of the damage. The Medical Examiner was unable to correctly identify whether she was Indian, Caucasian, or of Eskimo descent. A search of the crime scene revealed Walkman earphones near the body, but her ID was nowhere to be found. The fly section of her jeans had been deliberately cut out, and there was a single hair with no root on her stomach.

The student was immediately considered a suspect, and an interview was done at the police station. He stated that he had just done his finals, and decided to take a drive to clear his head when he spotted the body. His story sounded plausible, but since it had been raining at the time, investigators found it odd that he chose that time to take a scenic drive. To make sure all their bases were covered, they called the school and managed to confirm the student's story. This left them with no suspects, and the victim's identity was still unknown. They released various details to the media, hoping that someone would recognize the woman. The plan panned out.

Loretta Bennett called police, stating that she was worried about her 22-year-old daughter, Taunja Bennett. She hadn't seen Taunja in several days, and while this was not unlikely, her concern was growing. She told police that Taunja always had her Walkman with her, and that she was mentally challenged to some degree. Investigators asked her down to the station, and Loretta confirmed that the victim was her daughter Taunja. She explained that Taunja's mental issues made her naïve, and that she was a perfect victim. She didn't have a driver's license since she couldn't drive, and always took the bus or hitchhiked to her destinations. As investigators followed up on Taunja's movements, they discovered that she was last seen alive at the B&I Tavern in Portland. Since she was a frequent customer at the bar, the bartender and other patrons remembered seeing her in the bar for several hours. Several guys bought her beers, and she was last seen playing pool with two guys at the eastern end of the bar. No one saw her leaving, with the bartender stating that at one point he looked over to the pool table and saw that she was no longer there. However, the two men were still playing.

Despite the testimonies that Taunja hadn't left with the two men, investigators were still not convinced of their innocence. They theorized that the men could have met up with Taunja later, killed her and dumped her body. Unfortunately for the investigators, nobody seemed to know the identity of the two men. They had only been in the bar that one time, and hadn't been seen since. Police canvassed various bars and restaurants in the area, but there was no trace of either Taunja or the two men. It became clear that Taunja had disappeared shortly after leaving B&I Tavern.

Laverne Pavlinac and John Sosnovske

Two weeks after Taunja's body was found, the stalled investigation was revived after a woman called the police about the case. She stated that she had heard a man at a bar bragging about killing a young woman. Investigators followed up on the call and discovered that the tipster was a 50-something year old grandmother called Laverne Pavlinac. When they arrived at her house to follow up on her story, she changed her statement, telling them that she knew the man who was bragging. She stated that her boyfriend, 40-something year old John Sosnovske, had been intoxicated when he told her about killing a young woman and leaving her body in an embankment. She had then called the police with the tip. Pavlinac was a retired grandmother, and the investigators had a hard time believing that the nice, cordial woman was hanging out with murderers. According to Pavlinac, Sosnovske frequently got blackout drunk, and was in the habit of using her as a punching bag. Investigators wondered Sosnovske had tried the same with Taunja, but this time he had gone too far. With Pavlinac's statement in hand, investigators called Sosnovske in for an interview. He maintained that he had no idea what the investigators were talking about, and vehemently denied having anything to do with the murder. With no other evidence to support Pavlinac's statement, investigators had no choice but to release Sosnovske.

A week later, Pavlinac called investigators again, and this time she had more details to share. She told them that she had picked up Sosnovske at a truck stop on Sunday night, and that he was drunk. During the drive home, he told her that he had killed a young woman in the parking lot of the truck stop. He stated that he had choked her to death before placing her in the trunk of his friend's car, and that the friend had dumped the body in the embankment. With these new details, investigators felt like they needed to dig deeper for evidence to support Pavlinac's claims, so they obtained a search warrant for her home, which she shared with Sosnovske. After serving the warrant, investigators meticulously combed through each area of the home, and discovered rope in the storage area of the patio. The rope was similar to the one found tied around Taunja's neck. They also found a note inside a shoebox, and it read: "Taunja Bennett. Good Piece." The note led investigators to believe that Sosnovske had had a sexual encounter with Taunja, either consensually or against her will. Despite the possibley incriminatory evidence recovered, investigators were not satisfied. They had been specifically searching for the section cut out of Taunja's jeans, and they had not found it.

The next day, investigators received yet another call from Pavlinac. This time, she had even bigger news. She told them that she had found a purse in the trunk of her car, and that it didn't belong to her. Investigators rushed to the scene and recovered the purse. Inside, there was a cut section from a pair of jeans. This evidence was particularly incriminating, especially because investigators had never released the information about the cut section of Taunja's jeans. This information was only known by officers and the killer. To investigators, this meant that Sosnovske indeed had ties to the murder. When Sosnovske was brought in for questioning once again, he maintained his pleas of innocence, and even agreed to a polygraph. The results were inconclusive, and the polygraph examiner told investigators that Sosnovske was not telling the truth. They believed that he had killed Taunja, but they needed to analyze the evidence.

The hair found on Taunja's stomach was analyzed, and forensic experts maintained that it matched Sosnovske's. However, the investigation soon hit a snag. The section of jeans recovered from Pavlinac's car was made from different denim when it was compared to Taunja's jeans. Additionally, when she was shown the purse Pavlinac had discovered in her car, Loretta Bennett maintained that the purse was not her daughter's. Investigators were stunned. They confronted

Pavlinac about the evidence recovered in her car, and it wasn't long before she broke down and confessed to planting the evidence. As she cried, she insisted that she had only done it because Sosnovske was an evil person and that she wanted him caught. Investigators began doubting Pavlinac's credibility, but they had no choice but to admit that parts of her story were true.

Arrest and Conviction

The next day, investigators received another call from Pavlinac, who asked them down to her house. When they got there, they found a pot of coffee on the table. Pavlinac had a confession to make. She stated that she had been present when Sosnovske killed Taunja. The investigators were skeptical, but they sat and listened as she provided details of the crime. She stated that they had picked up Taunja at a truck stop about 20 miles from the B&I Tavern. They had driven her to Vista House, located on the Columbia Gorge. According to Pavlinac, Sosnovske had gotten Taunja out of the car and taken her to the stairwell in Vista House. There, on the steps, Sosnovske had raped and beaten Taunja, and that during the assault, she had pulled the rope tight against Taunja's neck, and pulled it until she died. This version of events shocked investigators since Pavlinac was now confessing to active participation in the murder. As she recounted the story, Pavlinac was visibly distraught. However, investigators maintained that they needed proof that Pavlinac was telling the truth. She agreed to show them where she and Sosnovske had dumped the body.

Pavlinac went with investigators to point out where they had dumped Taunja's body, and they had just passed the scene when she asked the driver to turn back. They turned around and headed westbound when Pavlinac asked them to stop the car. She got out and crossed the road, and as investigators watched her, she pointed to a spot in the embankment. Investigators were now convinced she had to be part of the murder since she had pointed at a spot less than 10 feet from where the body had actually been. Next, investigators went to Vista House to check out the stone steps Pavlinac had described in her statement. There, they found what appeared to be blood stains on the stairwell. Although typing couldn't be done on the samples, investigators were now inclined to believe Pavlinac's account of events. However, because of her age, general likeability, and her previous statements, investigators were having a hard time believing that she played such a huge role in Taunja's murder. So they called Pavlinac's daughter down to the station and told Pavlinac to tell her daughter about her involvement in the crime. Pavlinac didn't hesitate, and recounted the details of the murder, her daughter watching her in horror. This, investigators believed, was a great indication that Pavlinac was telling the truth.

Several days later, Pavlinac and Sosnovske were arrested and charged with murder. While Sosnovske still maintained his innocence, he revealed that he wasn't really sure whether he had committed the crime or not. He told investigators that he usually had total blackouts when he drank, and that he actually drank every night.

Pavlinac went on trial first. By this time, she had recanted her confession, but the prosecution didn't believe her because she had provided various details only the killer would have known. As the prosecution prepared for the trial, a peculiar message showed up on the walls of men's restrooms in two truck stops – in Umatilla, Oregon, and Livingston, Montana. The message read, "I killed Taunja Bennett, Portland, Oregon. Two people took the blame. I got away with it. Free to kill again. Buttons cut from jeans. Proof." While this pointed to the possibility of another killer, investigators were skeptical, suspecting that friends of Pavlinac and Sosnovske had written them to throw off the case. In February 1991, Pavlinac was convicted of Taunja's murder and sentenced to life in prison. Sosnovske decided not to risk a jury trial and possible death sentence. He took a plea of no contest, and was sentenced to serve life in prison.

The 'Happy Face Killer' Letters

In the fall of 1994, three years after Pavlinac and Sosnovske's convictions, the Portland Oregonian newspaper and the Washington County Judges Criminal Court received bizarre letters that seemed to take the Taunja Bennett case into a whole new direction. The anonymous writer claimed that Pavlinac and Sosnovske were innocent, and that he was the one who killed Taunja. He added that Taunja was just the first of his many victims. He revealed that he was a long haul trucker, but that he had wanted to quit at some point because of how easy it was to find victims. He claimed that he wanted to stop killing, and that he had killed five women in total. He stated that killing thrilled him, and even though he thought he would stop killing after he murdered Taunja, two years later, he killed a woman in California. He then went on to kill again and again. At the top of the letter, the writer had drawn a smiley face, which earned him the nickname "The Happy Face Killer."

Investigators reacted to the letters cautiously, believing that it could be a hoax. This was not the first time someone else was claiming to be Taunja's killer, and the messaging in the letter was similar to the writings found in the restrooms. However, investigators couldn't let go of their suspicions that someone was trying to tamper with Pavlinac and Sosnovske's sentences, or the author of the letter was just looking for attention. However, since the letters contained detailed descriptions of various murders, investigators began the painstaking process of determining whether the crimes described had actually occurred. Fingerprint and DNA samples were recovered from the letters, but investigators found no matches. This ruled out Pavlinac and Sosnovske as the authors, but offered no further information on who it could be.

However, investigators were able to match up the details of a murder in California to the account of events described in the letter.

The Murder of Julie Ann Winningham

On March 10, 1995, the nude body of Julie Ann Winningham was discovered lying over an embankment in the woods in Washougal, Washington, just over the Oregon State line. She had been sexually assaulted, strangled, and dumped off the highway. As investigators in Clark County began investigating Winningham's murder, they quickly found out that she was a frequent presence in the local bars. As they interviewed the bartender who saw her on the night of her murder, he explained that she had been alone that night, although she was seeing someone on and off. He stated that the man was a trucker. With no further pertinent information received from canvassing the bars, investigators took a deeper look into Winnigham's life. They found out that she had recently sold her car, and that the bill of sale had been written up by a man called Keith Hunter Jesperson, who had also served as the witness. Investigators found out that Jesperson had no prior arrests and no history of violence.

Investigators reached out to Jesperson for an interview, and he willingly came down to the station. He stated that he was a long haul trucker, and that he was Winningham's fiancé. He stated that the last time he had seen her, they had been arguing in the cab of his truck when she grabbed her belongings and left. He let her be, and maintained that he knew nothing of her murder. However, investigators found it odd that Jesperson never asked how Winningham died, and didn't seem upset by the news of her murder. After a five-hour interview, investigators let him go. They had taken hair and blood samples from Jesperson, and processed the inside of his truck. With nothing to detain him, one investigator handed Jesperson his card and asked him to call if he thought of anything else.

Confession and Link to 'The Happy Face Killer'

That same evening following his interview, Jesperson picked up the investigator's card and called the number on it. When he identified himself, the investigator was surprised. Jesperson stated that he wanted to confess to Winningham's murder and then he hung up. Stunned, the investigator relayed this news to his colleagues. When Jesperson showed up at the station, he was more than willing to talk. He told the investigators that he was nervous he was being followed around, so he decided to confess. He stated that after having sex with Winningham, she had asked him for money and he refused. She then stated that she was going to get him charged with rape. Outraged, he put his fist to her throat and duct taped her mouth shut so she couldn't continue yelling at him. He stated that she stopped breathing, and that was when he realized she was dead. He took her body to a turnout on the highway and threw her over the embankment.

While he was in county jail, Jesperson wrote a letter to his brother, which was in turn obtained by the media, making headline news. The letter, dated March 24, 1995, read in part:

Hi Brad,

Seems like my luck has run out. I got into a bad situation and got caught up with emotion. I killed a woman in my truck during an argument. I'm sure they will kill me for this. I'm sorry that this turned out this way, I've been a killer for five years and I've killed eight people and assaulted more."

Investigators in Clark County knew Jesperson had only been arrested for one murder, so they began looking into his claims that he had killed eight people. The letter to his brother had become sensational news, and they were fielding calls from media, many wondering if they had any leads about any other potential victims. One Portland journalist, however, had something different to tell them. He told a Clark County investigator about the Happy Face Killer letters, and stated that he had found a connection between the letters and the information they had on Jesperson at the time. Jesperson, on his part, was busy telling other inmates about the other murders he had committed, including the locations of the crimes and where the bodies were dumped. The details he provided matched up with the information detailed in the Happy Face Killer's letters. This information was relayed to the Portland investigators, who quickly became aware of the similarities between the murders of Taunja Bennett and Julie Ann Winningham. Using the information from the Happy Face Killer letters, Portland investigators called the Nebraska authorities to tell them about a body along the Interstate, and asked them to recover it, which they did.

With the possible identity of the Happy Face Killer now known, forensic experts compared the fingerprint and DNA samples recovered from the letters to Jesperson's. They matched, proving beyond doubt that Jesperson did author the letters. They also confirmed cases in California, Wyoming, and Florida, linking them to Jesperson. However, his claims that he had murdered Taunja Bennett made investigators skeptical, but they started looking for concrete proof to either incriminate or exclude Jesperson, since there were two people in jail for the crime. They ascertained that Jesperson was indeed in the area when Taunja went missing.

Indisputable Evidence

As Portland investigators tried looking for proof that Jesperson did indeed kill Taunja Bennett, Jesperson kept pushing his defense lawyer to convince police that Pavlinac and Sosnovske were innocent, and that he indeed killed her. With every single piece of evidence still incriminating Pavlinac and Sosnovske, investigators asked Jesperson whether he could produce concrete evidence pointing to his guilt. Seemingly like an afterthought, Jesperson asked if showing them where he threw her purse would be enough proof. Investigators affirmed that it would be a good start. Jesperson led the investigators to an area on the sandy river and stated that he threw Taunja's ID and the contents of her purse in the area. Coupled with the fact that it had been five years since the murder, there were overgrown blackberry bushes covering the entire area, which made it difficult for investigators to start the search.

Explorer scouts were called in, and after cutting down the bushes, were unable to find the supposed evidence. However, unwilling to give up, one investigator asked the team to search about six inches into the ground because of the years that had passed. When the scouts went back, they dug a few inches into the ground and found Taunja's laminated Portland ID, what was left of her purse, and its contents. This was definitive proof that Jesperson was Taunja Bennett's killer.

The day following the discovery, investigators began the process of getting Pavlinac and Sosnovske out of jail. When Pavlinac was asked why she made up the story of killing Taunja, she stated that she had been tired of Sosnovske, and just wanted him out of her life. At the time, Taunja's murder seemed like the perfect opportunity. When asked how she knew about the piece of jeans, she stated that it had been listed in the search warrant investigators handed to her. Every other information she gave about the case was just from basic deduction and lucky guesses.

When asked about Taunja's murder, Jesperson stated that on the afternoon she went missing, he had been in the B&I Tavern for a few hours when he noticed her. He left for a while, and when he came back, he found her in the parking lot. He asked her to dinner, and she agreed. However, they first stopped at his rented home for sex when something went wrong. According to Jesperson, Taunja said something like, "Let's get it over with," adding that she was hungry. He flew into a rage and started punching her face, then strangled her. He stated that beat her so badly that there was blood splattered on the ceiling. He cut of the fly section of her jeans so that he wouldn't leave fingerprints. His plan was to commit the perfect murder that he had read about in a detective magazine.

Victims

· Taunja Bennett was his first victim, killed in Portland, Oregon, on January 22, 1990. He strangled her with a rope, beat her in the face 20 times, and dumped her body in an embankment.

· Claudia (name provided by Jesperson, although her identity remains unknown) was raped and killed in Blythe, California, on August 30, 1992.

· Cynthia Lyn Rose was killed by manual strangulation in Turlock, California, in 1992. She was 32 at the time.

· 26-year-old Laurie Ann Pentland was strangled with an unspecified ligature in Salem, Oregon, in November 1992.

· Carla/Cindy (identity unknown; name provided by Jesperson) died of unknown causes in July 1993.

· 40-year-old Susanne was killed in Crestview, Florida, on September 14, 1994. Her cause of death remains unknown.

· 21-year-old Angela Surbrize was killed in Spokane, Washington, in January 1995. She had been raped, manually strangled, and then tied to a truck and dragged post-mortem.

· 41-year-old Julie Ann Winningham, Jeperson's fiancée and his last victim, was killed by manual strangulation in Washougal, Washington, on March 10, 1995.

Despite his letter confession claiming he had killed eight people, Jesperson has claimed to have committed to up to 185 murders, although these claims have yet to be proven.

Convictions

Keith Hunter Jesperson was sentenced to serve three consecutive life terms in Oregon State Penitentiary, Salem. He was indicted for murder in September 2009 and was extradited to Riverside County, California in December. He received a fourth life term in January 2010.

LAUREN STUART

In 2017, Lauren Stuart looked to be living the picture-perfect life in Keego Harbor, Michigan. Her husband Dan doted on her daily, providing a nice home for her and their two children. Working as a data solutions architect for the University of Michigan's Center for Integrative Research in Critical Care, he possessed an IQ of over 165. To top it off, their two children, Stephen and Bethany were well on their way to becoming well-adjusted adults. Stephen was following in his father's footsteps, becoming well-versed in computer science while Bethany took the artistic route, earning a scholarship in graphic design.

All the while, however, the family was beholden to the Jehovah's Witness Church.

Dan wanted more for his children than he had. He didn't graduate from college and felt as if that held him back in his career. He wanted his children to have more options than he had. Making plans for both of their children to attend college, Dan didn't realize that the Jehovah Witness sect to which he belonged frowned greatly on pursuing higher education. When word got back to the church elders, one of the elders called the entire Stuart family into the back room of the church where they received an "education."

"You don't need college," the elder lectured the family. "You're going to be exposed to pernicious levels of immorality. Sex, drugs and God knows whatever else."

"They (the church elders) could be really intimidating," a former Jehovah's Witness member said. "It would have started off polite. They always started off that way. But any back talk was greeted with an icy silence before quoting some scripture. They would shame you into doing things their way."

But the stern warning did nothing to dissuade Dan from sending his children to college. The church elders responded by "shunning" the Stuarts. This "shunning" or expulsion from the church affected the family a great deal, extracting an emotional toll on the couple.

"It hurt Lauren particularly hard," forensic psychologist Paula Orange said. "She had spent her entire life in that church. It was like the rug was pulled out from under her."

"They were shunned every way possible," said Joyce Taylor, a family friend, and former Jehovah's Witness. "If Lauren went to the grocery store, they didn't look her in the eye. When you are raised a Jehovah's Witness, they choose your friends. They choose who you associate with. And if you go against that, they will dis-fellowship you, or shun you."

Lauren coped initially by busying herself with improvements around the home. She replaced the roof, painted the house and furnished the kitchen all on her own.

This "hyperactivity" did little to stem her raising depression, however.

In the small town of Keego Harbor, being shunned from the church was almost akin to getting the cold shoulder from the community at large. At least that is what it must have felt like. People they had known for years refused to acknowledge them in public. The friends of their children stopped returning their calls.

Without the church, the family's social life turned to zero.

But Lauren decided to change that.

Seeking a new life, Lauren looked into the prospect of becoming a model and actress. She was concerned about her age but found that the industry was open to fit models like herself.

"I love acting and modeling," Lauren wrote in her online modeling portfolio. "I am a very passionate person and it reflects in my work. I am adventurous in nature and so I like a wide variety of acting and modeling experiences. I enjoy learning new things, especially with good direction. ... Life is an adventure and my goal is to die knowing I did the things I wanted to do."

Lauren enrolled at the local John Casablancas modeling studio and immediately caught the eye of the director, Bernadette Strickland.

"I remember her because she had enrolled in our workshops," Strickland said. "She was very nice. She asked a lot of questions. She looked like she had a great family and she was very attractive. She kept herself up so well."

Lauren would dabble in modeling but gave it up after only a few shoots. Some of the photos are mildly provocative with Lauren wearing only a sheer gown in some shots.

A fitness freak, she also became a personal trainer at the local YMCA and cleaned houses for spare cash.

She never lost faith in the church, however. Lauren began researching Jehovah Witness literature on her own.

"She went nuts on it," a family friend recalled. "She became obsessed with end times. Armaggedon. She no longer attended the church but she became even more obsessed with it."

"Lauren couldn't escape the psychosis of the church," Orange said. "Jehovah's Witness teach that when Armageddon comes and you're alive, you'll be destroyed with all the other wicked people. This propelled Lauren into a deep depression."

But judging from Lauren's Youtube channel, she appears to have broken off from the direct teachings of the church. She liked the teachings of *normal* Evangelical speakers like Ravi Zacharias. It appears, however, that she became obsessed with "end times" and "prophecy" conspiracists.

Taking these teachings literally, Lauren decided to take matters into her own hands. She made the decision to kill her family then herself.

But she showed no sign of trouble to those close to her.

"She came over to my house. we had tea, coffee and talked," her friend Joyce Taylor recalled. "Lauren talked about her kids and expressed excitement about her husband being involved in a project at the University of Michigan, where, she said, he was helping develop a software program that helps detect heart attacks. She was talking about the business he was hoping to get going, how much she was looking forward to it. We talked about that, our kids."

Like a lot of people suffering from mental illness, she did an excellent job of hiding the disease from others. She went on trips with her husband. They toured Old Virginia. Maui.

Lauren smiled through it all until it came to be too much.

By 2017, she was researching suicide methods on Youtube. Swallowing pills. Poison. Slicing wrists.

Settling on a self-inflicted gunshot, she began researching guns. Lauren decided that the Glock handgun would be the quickest way to go.

Lauren then posted two videos on her Youtube channel. She verbalized how "broken" she was and how she didn't want to be a burden on her family. She also briefly touched on the sexual abuse she suffered in a follow-up video the next day. "I'm on a path to destruction," she said.

Taking pen in hand, she detailed her reasons further in a suicide note which she left on the dinner table. Lauren then cleaned up the house one last time. She texted her cousin with the message "I took my husband and kids with me so they don't have to feel my selfish act. They will sleep until Christ resurrects them. I truly hope you do better where I have failed."

"Lauren, you are scaring me?" her cousin texted back. What are u saying?????...Don't do it Lauren."

Bethany was the first to go. Lauren crept behind her daughter who was napping in her bedroom. She placed a pillow on her head before firing twice, suppressing the noise.

Then her son Stephen came home. She had texted him asking if he "was still coming over to the house."

"Hi Mom," he said, cheerfully coming through the door. "Is Bethany home?"

"She's asleep," Lauren said. "But could you help with my computer? I think it has a virus?"

Stephen complied, walking into the family computer room and sitting himself down on the desk chair, swiveling around.

"Okay, so what's up?" he said, spinning around before seeing his own mother pointing the Glock at him.

"Mom?

She fired, killing her son instantly.

Lauren then paced around the home, waiting for Danny to arrive. She turned over all of the photos of her family, making sure she didn't see their smiling faces.

Lauren texted her husband's boss. "Mark, this is Lauren. Dad had a accident this morning and has died. I can't talk now. Someone will inform you later on details at the hospital."

Dan's supervisor immediately texted back but received no response.

Catching her husband unaware in the basement, Lauren shot him to death.

Finally, she killed the dog.

A neighbor heard the gunshot but thought it was someone "slamming doors."

The bodies were discovered the next morning by police. Her cousin had arrived earlier and went over to the house. When no one answered the door, she called the authorities to do a welfare check.

The police entered the home and found it to be a tidy one. The kitchen was clean, the refrigerator filled with food.

They found the dog first.

"Get your gun out," the officer called out, believing that an active shooter was present. "There's a dead dog in the tub."

Ascending the spiral staircase to the second floor, they found Steven's body next. Face down on the floor of the spare bedroom. He had been shot twice. In the adjoining bedroom, they found Bethany. A bloodied pillow remained over her head.

Dan had been found in the basement. He had been shot in front of the couch. Investigators noted that his right hand had remained in the front pocket of his jeans and the white pocket liner was slightly pulled out from the left pocket, with the assumption being he was standing up while he was shot, hands in his pockets.

An unsuspecting victim attempting to hold up his hands...

Lauren was found at the bottom of the basement stairwell. A gunshot entry almost perfectly placed between her eyes.

She had researched this online. The foolproof way to kill oneself.

She had left two letters on the dinner table. She addressed the Medical Examiner in one. The other was a suicide note.

"I allowed evil into my heart when I chose not to accept God's free love and it made me sick inside," Lauren wrote. "I killed my family because I know my death would stumble them. At least now they will not suffer and will be resurrected into love forever in peace."

The rest of the letter has remained sealed under police orders.

Interviews by police conducted after the murder/suicide painted a different picture of what they presented. Family members, friends and neighbors all described the Stuarts as "quiet but odd."

Lauren had eleven siblings but struggled with depression, presumably the after effect of the alleged sexual abuse she suffered at the hands of an unknown relative. This depression worsened after she had a family of her own.

"They interviewed Lauren's dad," Orange said. "But he had not spoken to her in several years. Evidently, her mother died of cancer when she was only thirteen."

Additionally, Dan and Lauren's father never saw eye to eye.

"He pulled Lauren away from the family," Lauren's father was quoted as saying.

One of Lauren's sisters repeated the line, believing that Dan was the reason that no one in their family saw Lauren in years. She believed that they both suffered from the same mental illness.

"She worshiped Danny," family friend Joyce Taylor said. "Danny worshiped her. They were like hand in glove. But she was very concerned about Dan. He was prone to depression and she was always worried about him."

Interestingly, there were small traces of marijuana found in her system after the autopsy as well as in Dan and Steven.

On Dan's Youtube channel, you wouldn't guess he was a Jehovah's Witness. He looks to have made the transition to Evangelical Christianity much like his wife judging by the videos he shared. He shared a video by the Evangelical preacher Hugh Ross, who like Ravi Zacharias, was a Christian apologist and the furthest thing from a Jehovah's Witness. Dan also displays a love for the heavy metal band Metallica (which would have been frowned upon by the JWs), sailboats, and Dodge Challengers. He also shared numerous videos from a Hawaii trip that he and his wife enjoyed in 2015. During these videos, there is no sign of any manic depression from either party. They look to be a normal couple, even fun-loving couple as evidenced by a video which shows Lauren enjoying a ride on a mechanical bull. She laughs uncontrollably and gives no indication of a future murder/suicide.

"It is clear that Lauren showed symptoms of severe depression and displayed abnormal behavior leading up to the incident," the police report read. "It would appear that Lauren immersed herself in her own world of her version of religion and increased depression. Lauren's' complete immersion into religion appeared to have only further alienated her and her family from friends and other families which may have compounded her already fragile state of mind."

During an interview with authorities, police noted that one of her sisters expressed little emotion or surprise at the murder/suicide.

"(The sister) showed a very solemn and somber demeanor when she spoke," the police report stated. "She stated that she is not sad for Lauren and her family and that when she heard the news of her sister's actions, she was not surprised in the slightest."

Family friend Joyce Taylor blamed the church. She addressed a Jehovah's Witness meeting shortly after the murders and blasted the parishioners.

"Excuse me, everyone, My name is Joyce Taylor," she yelled. "Two days ago, four people died as a result of your shunning process. Five years ago you people pulled your support from this small family, the only support they had was you people. You turned them away and you shunned them. For what?!! Because they wanted to raise their children as they saw fit."

The crime would make it the third such incident in two decades of murder/suicide in families that have been shunned from the Jehovah's Witnesses. In 2001, Christian Longo murdered his wife and three children in Oregon after the church shunned him. In 2014, a South Carolina father murdered his wife and three children after being shunned...

But another family friend believed that the shunning of the church did not spur Lauren to do the murder/suicide. The shunning had occurred years prior and Lauren struggled with mental illness her entire life.

"This is a tragedy that has to do with a disease," the friend stated. "Depression is so prevalent, and when it goes untreated this is what happens. She needed medical help."

Joyce Taylor would later admit that Lauren's preoccupation with Armaggedon disturbed her.

"It's the end times," Lauren would say to her. "I know it is."

The conjecture here is that the family's shunning at the hands of the Jehovah's Witness had little to do with the ultimate murder/suicide as the timeline doesn't match up. The eldest child, Steven, was twenty-seven at the time of the murder in 2018. So the family's expulsion from the church must have been around 2009 or 2010 as that would have been the time in which he entered college. That is a minimum of eight years apart from the church during which time the family seemed to have moved on from the strict teachings of the JW's.

This is not a defense of the Jehovah's Witness teaching but in judging some of the media reports the church appears to have been a convenient scapegoat for something unexplainable. They both turned to Evangelical Christianity after the shunning. But there is a faction "regular" Christianity that spends an inordinate amount of time focused on biblical prophecy in regards to end times. These are rabbit hole conversations and thought processes that both Dan and Lauren were certainly susceptible to, considering their mental states.

During their 2015 Hawaii vacation videos, the couple seems relaxed. Dan doesn't say much of anything throughout the videos and Lauren does the talking. She looks haggard and considerably older than her appearance in the 2012 photos. Her face is creased and she looks all of forty-seven years old. But the bright smile is still there, leaving no indication that a murder/suicide was only three years away.

Lauren's disturbing video (which has since been taken down) is evidence that she lays the blame on herself. She wanted to kill herself and overthought the process, wanting to spare her children and spouse over the grief of her suicide. So in her warped thinking, she took their lives and even that of the family dog before taking her own.

THE BRILLIANT SERIAL KILLER : THE TRUE STORY OF ISRAEL KEYES

MARK TOLBERT

Israel Keyes was an American serial killer who was active from approximately 2001 to his capture in 2012. He was known for his extreme attention to detail, his patience and discipline in selecting targets that lived far away from him. He was also meticulous in disposing of his victim's bodies as authorities have not uncovered any other evidence that Keyes did not provide.

Keyes killed several victims across the United States and was finally caught in 2012 after he uncharacteristically deviated from his modus operandi and hatched a plan to collect a ransom from his last victim's family.

Keyes was known to go to extreme lengths to hide his involvement in these murders, including driving across the country in rental cars, while using nothing but cash and removing the batteries from his cell phones in order to evade detection. This is uncharacteristic for a serial killer, since the vast majority of his contemporaries are known to have killed within their general geographic area.

While in federal custody in Anchorage, Alaska, Keyes would cooperate with investigators and admit to a host of crimes, including kidnapping, rape, and murder. Furthermore, Keyes admitted to committing a variety of burglaries and bank robberies to fund his killing sprees.

Early Life

Israel Keyes was born in Richmond, Utah in 1978. He was the second child to John Jeffrey Keyes and Heidi Hokansson. John, a maintenance man, and Heidi, a stay-at-home mom, raised their son in a Mormon environment and home-schooled both Israel and his eight siblings.

Soon after his birth, Israel's parents moved the family to Aladdin Road, a small area north of Colville, Washington. While his family officially followed the Mormon faith, they were known to attend a local Christian Identity church, an organization rumored follow a white supremacist version of Christianity. Some, however, dispute this label and liken the religion to having parallels with the Amish church.

The family also quickly became friends with the neighbors, the Kehoe family. Chevie Kehoe, the eldest of eight sons, would later become an infamous white supremacist and convicted murderer, after killing William Frederick Mueller, along with his wife and daughter, during a robbery to secure guns, ammunition, and money.

During his time in Aladdin Road, Israel became a very introverted child with little interaction with the other children in town. He built his own cabin at the age of sixteen and preferred the wilderness over people. He is known to have burglarized several houses during his time in Aladdin, however, and is believed to have killed family pets for entertainment.

"When I was fourteen there was some friends staying with us," Keyes recalled. "And there was this cat of ours that was always getting into the trash. I had a lot of guns and I would always carry a gun and I shot it in the stomach. And it ran around and around the tree...and then it like crashed into the tree. I actually kind of laughed a little I think but..and then I looked over at everybody else and the kid who was with me, he was throwing up. Like he was, really, I don't know (chuckles) traumatized I guess you would say."

"Like most serial killers," forensic psychiatrist Paula Orange said. "Keyes built himself up to killing people by killing small animals first."

Following his family's relocation to Smyrna, Maine to become involved in the maple syrup business in the late 1990s, Keyes was kicked out of his family home for rejecting his parents' faith. His parents told his siblings to stay away from him.

"Keyes didn't think too much of his family," Orange said. "He was raised in a cult-like atmosphere and rejected the family religion, becoming very outspoken out his lack of belief in God. He had a Satanic pentagram branded on his back as well as an upside-down cross on his chest."

The rejection made Keyes want to tour the country and burn down as many churches as he could. Instead, he turned to murder and rape.

His first violent crime was committed sometime between 1996 and 1998, when Keyes abducted a teenage girl and raped her. Despite his later penchant for murder, he allowed this victim to go free. The identity of the teenage girl remains unknown.

Military Career

In 1998, Israel Keyes decided to enlist in the United States Army while living in New Jersey. Keyes served as a specialist in the 1st Battalion, 5th Infantry. He was subsequently stationed at Ft. Lewis, near Tacoma, Washington, and at Ft. Hood, near Killeen, Texas. He would later receive training in the Sinai region of Egypt.

While serving in the U.S. Army, Keyes was awarded the Army Achievement Medal for "meritorious service while assigned as a gunner and assistant gunner from the 2nd of December 1998 to the 8th of July, 2001 in the Alpha Company 60mm mortar section." Although Keyes received a DUI in Washington state in May 2001, he left the U.S. Army with an honorable discharge later that year.

Keyes would settle in Alaska and get a job working in construction. Incredibly, he would draw rave reviews from his employer who had no idea of the double life his new carpenter with the long hair led.

"Keyes was described as someone who was very professional," Orange said. "He had a tremendous focus and would work on projects for hours on end with intensity and focus. He would not stop for lunch. He would just work straight on through."

Keyes was described in a favorable manner by just about everyone else who met him. Words like "friendly", "low-key", "reliable" were among the adjectives used to describe him.

"The secret life was power to Israel Keyes," Orange said. "He got off on the fact that everyone he encountered had no idea who or what he really was. To them, he was a friendly carpenter who was on the quiet side. Mellow. But inside he was a raging killer. That is what gave him power."

Crimes

Bill & Lorraine Currier

After receiving his honorable discharge from the United States Army, and sometime between April and May 2011, Israel Keyes constructed a homemade silencer for his Ruger .22 pistol. Once he decided to kill, Keyes booked a flight from Washington state to Indiana. After arriving in Indiana, Keyes rented a car and drove the remaining 1,000 miles to the East Coast of the United States, using cash-only for the duration of the trip to avoid leaving behind any evidence.

Keyes arrived in New York to test his homemade silencer, then traveled to Vermont to pick up a murder "toolkit" that he had buried two years before. Keyes soon found an abandoned farmhouse in Essex, Vermont, which he identified as the location he would take his next victim to before killing them. He initially targeted random drivers passing through the rural area, intending to shoot out a tire on their car and kidnap them after they crashed, but decided to focus on a married couple after dismissing his original plan as unpractical and dangerous.

He soon identified Bill and Lorraine Currier, living at 8 Colbert Street, as his next victims on July 8, 2011.

Bill and Lorraine were 49 and 55 years old respectively. They had just celebrated their 25th wedding anniversary. Bill worked at the local university as a lab assistant while Lorraine worked at a nearby medical center.

"They were good people," Orange said. "They had a lot of pride in the upkeep of their Vermont home, manicuring the lawn and planting flowers. They were good employees and well-liked by co-workers. They were the epitome of upstanding, normal good people."

Keyes had picked the Currier's because they had no dog, no kids and a garage that would let him into the house. He stalked them for days, knowing their comings and going.

As one investigator would note, "Keyes was a serial killer with a system."

In the middle of the night, Keyes disabled the Currier's phone line and entered their house in what has been described as a "blitz attack." He ambushed the couple while they were sleeping and quickly subdued them, tying the couple up and stealing Lorraine's .38 snub-nose revolver in the process.

Once the couple was secured, he proceeded to transport them to the abandoned farmhouse in Essex. During the course of the night, both Lorraine and Bill attempted to escape the house. Lorraine was successfully captured and re-restrained. However, Keyes shot Bill with his silenced .22 caliber Ruger pistol in a fit of rage during his escape attempt. After killing Bill, Keyes sexually assaulted Lorraine and strangled her to death in the basement.

Following the killings, Keyes buried Bill and Lorraine's bodies in the basement of the Essex farmhouse, intending to return to the house at a later date to set fire to the building and thereby destroy any evidence in the blaze. Once the bodies were buried, Keyes set out to commit a robbery spree using the Currier's car.

"Keyes was spotted driving the Currier's car," Orange said. "The eyewitness quickly relayed this information to the police and they were able to come up with a sketch of Keyes. They were reported missing by this time and the authorities knew that foul play was involved. Things became particularly worrisome as the man in Currier's car was driving alone and the couple was nowhere to be found."

The Currier's car soon suffered "serious mechanical issues" and Keyes decided not to go through with his crime spree.

Keyes quickly abandoned the Currier's non working car in an apartment parking lot at 203 Pearl Street and proceeded to the White National Monument Forest to burn the couple's belongings and to bury his toolkit and handgun.

Unbeknownst to Keyes, the farmhouse containing the Currier's bodies was bulldozed from October 25-27, 2011. The bodies, along with the rest of the farmhouse, were unknowingly disposed of at the local landfill.

The resting place lived up to Keyes' motto, 'Out of sight, out of mind.'

Samantha Koenig

On February 1, 2012, Keyes began to search for another random victim. He identified 18-year old barista Samantha Koenig, living and working in Anchorage, Alaska, as his next victim.

Samantha worked at a walk-up kiosk on a relatively busy highway. It was snowing that night, however, and folks were driving by too fast to pay attention to the man who walked up to the counter in a ski mask. This would not be unusual in Anchorage as the weather was freezing. Samantha greeted Israel with a smile and he handed her his travel mug, asking for some coffee. She would turn back around he had a gun pointed at her.

"Turn out the lights," he commanded.

Samantha complied.

"Turn around," he said.

Samantha began to cry, complying with his command. He forced her to empty the register then tied up her wrists with cable wire. After finding out that Koenig had a boyfriend who was set to show up soon, Keyes laid in wait for the boyfriend, Duane Tortolani. However, he quickly abandoned his plan to capture a second victim and dragged Koenig to his truck before transporting her to his property.

The next day, February 2nd, Keyes broke into Koenig's house. While there, he also burglarized her boyfriend's truck, taking the couple's joint debit card with him. However, both Koenig's father and Duane Tortolani witnessed this burglary and notified the authorities.

Keyes quickly tested the debit card to make sure that it worked and, upon confirming that it worked, he returned to his home and quickly killed Koenig, leaving her body in a storage shed located on his property. He immediately traveled to New Orleans, where he set out on a week-long cruise. However, once he disembarked from the cruise Keyes became increasingly concerned over the media coverage and intense police investigation of Keonig's disappearance and set out on a crime spree.

On February 16, Keyes burglarized and burned down a home in Aledo, Texas. Shortly thereafter, Keyes robbed the National Bank of Texas, attempting to kidnap yet another woman he saw walking a dog. Luckily, this potential victim was able to escape.

Other Victims

Israel Keyes is suspected of killing or attempting to kill several other victims. Keyes' first admitted violent crime took place sometime between 1996 and 1998, when he abducted and raped a teenage girl in Washington state. Unlike his later crimes, Keyes did not kill this victim. He released her soon after the sexual assault.

"My entire goal was to stay under the radar," Keyes said. "For a lot of this stuff, there wasn't anything. All I can say is that unless I talk about it, you're never going to find any evidence."

His first suspected murder is of an unknown couple in Washington State in 2001. Keyes also claimed to have killed another unidentified victim in Leah Bay, Washington in July 2001.

He planned out his killings like most people plan out their vacations. He would travel far away from his location.

From 2005 to 2006, Keyes is suspected of killing two separate victims. He confessed to these murders while being held at the

Anchorage Correctional Complex, saying that these murders were committed on two separate occasions. Furthermore, he claimed to have dumped one of the bodies in Crescent Lake, located in Oregon.

"There is a history of this stuff that goes back a long time," Keyes said. "It's not something I've ever talked to anyone about."

Keyes just didn't rape his female victims. He would rape his male victims as well. It was something he was ashamed of as well as his necrophilia.

Following a multi-year break from killing, Keyes admitted to killing Debra J. Feldman in Hackensack, New Jersey on April 8, 2009. He also claimed to have killed another victim the following day somewhere in New York state.

Keyes would bury his murder weapons across numerous fields across the entire United States. Because of his military training, he knew how to maintain the weapons and return to them after they had been out of use for years. He buried these weapons in canisters filled with cable ties, ropes and drain cleaner.

During these trips, Keyes would admit to frequenting prostitutes.

Lastly, following the murder of Samantha Koenig and during his travels throughout the Southwestern United States, Keyes claims to have killed an unknown victim in Texas. The identity and final location of this victim remain unknown.

In addition to the actual murders that he committed, Keyes admitted to attempting to kill several other individuals over the years. For example, Keyes admitted to attempting to shoot both a couple and male police officer in Anchorage, Alaska sometime between April and May 2011. He also admitted to attempting to kidnap and kill a woman he spotted walking her dog in Texas, just days before his capture by a combination of Texas and federal law enforcement.

Other Crimes

Keyes was known to commit burglaries and bank robberies in order to fund his killing sprees. In addition, he admitted to killing small animals from the time he was a young child. He is said to have killed an unknown number of family dogs and cats throughout his travels.

<u>April 10, 2009</u>

Keyes robbed the Community Bank in Tupper Lake, NY in order to fund his killing spree. After holding up the bank teller with a .40 caliber Smith & Wesson (and with a .22 caliber 10/22 Ruger pistol in reserve), Keyes made off with over $10,000 in cash. Although he was filmed on camera during the robbery, his use of sunglasses, uncharacteristic clothing, and a fake mustache prevented him from being identified.

Following the successful robbery, Keyes buried a box with his robbery supplies in the Woodside Natural Area in Essex, Utah. He returned home four days later with the $10,000 in his possession.

<u>February 16, 2012</u>

While Keyes was traversing across the Southwestern United States following the successful ransom for Samantha Koenig, he committed two additional crimes. First, Keyes committed arson by setting fire to and burning down a 3,500 square foot house in Aledo, Texas. Secondly, Keyes again committed a bank robbery by holding up a teller at the National Bank of Texas in Azle, Texas, making off with an undisclosed amount of cash.

In all, Keyes is suspected of committing some 20 to 30 home invasions and burglaries during his lifetime. Furthermore, he killed an unknown amount of animals from his childhood to capture and is believed to have committed several unidentified bank robberies during his adult years in order to fund his killing trips across the country.

Capture

After murdering Samantha Koenig and leaving Alaska, Keyes concocted a plan to demand a $30,000 ransom for Koenig's return (at the time, police were unaware that Koenig had been killed). Keyes texted his demands and instructions to Duane Tortolani, Koenig's boyfriend.

At the same time, Keyes dug up the body of Samantha Koenig, dismembered it, and disposed of the body in Matanuska Lake.

The case became a high-profile one and community members chipped in to meet the ransom demand.

Thirty-thousand dollars, courtesy of a concerned and frightened community, would be deposited into Samantha's account.

After receiving the ransom money, Keyes began withdrawing cash from the associated account using her stolen debit card. There would be withdrawals in Alaska. Then Arizona. Then New Mexico.

The authorities would always be fifteen minutes behind the suspect when he made these withdrawals.

Israel would wear a "Scream" mask while the withdrawals but his 2012 Ford Focus that he was drawing was identified. The FBI noted all of their counterparts to be on the lookout for Keyes in this vehicle. It is important to note that Keyes actually exchanged his rented 2012 Ford Focus for another car to avoid detection; however, the rental company provided him with another 2012 Ford Focus for his exchange. This would eventually help to lead to his capture.

Police were then able to track account withdrawals as he traveled throughout the Southwestern United States, having made withdrawals from Koenig's account using her debit card in New Mexico, Arizona, and Texas. Interestingly, authorities had a video of Koenig's abduction but refused to release the footage to the public, a controversial move that many outsiders saw as hampering his capture.

Having left his sister's wedding just days before (where he became embroiled in a contentious argument about his pronounced atheism), Keyes was spotted speeding along Highway 59 by a Texas Highway Patrolman on March 13, 2012.

"The patrolman that made the traffic stop had no idea that Keyes was a wanted serial killer," Orange said "Keyes did not have his gun handy at the time. If he had, there's no doubt in my mind that he would have started shooting."

Keyes was placed under arrest by the patrolman and the Texas Rangers as well as the FBI was brought in. Authorities found the following items in Keyes' possession at the time of his capture: Koenig's ATM card and cell phone (with the battery removed), a ski-mask, handgun, and bundles of rubber-banded cash that was traced to the recent National Bank of Texas robbery.

The authorities still had hope that Samantha was still alive.

But Keyes would tell them nothing. He stared straight ahead without emotion as detectives hammered him with questions. Authorities would get very little out of him. He was thirty-four years old and lived a quiet life with his girlfriend and ten year old daughter in Anchorage. Everything about Keyes' past seemed normal. But he had a creepy withdrawn nature about his personality. When the FBI searched his property, they found out why.

He had searched numerous time on his computer for Samantha Koenig. The FBI would then confront Keyes with the surveillance footage they had of his truck pulling up in front of the kiosk.

"We know it was your truck," the FBI agent said.

Keyes would remain silent for about forty seconds before he finally spoke.

"Well, I might as well tell you everything. She's dead."

Keyes revealed that he had used a needle and thread to open up Samantha's eyes as she posed with the newspaper in the ransom photo.

Keyes would recount how he brought Samantha back to his home and tied her up. He had a glass of wine before he began verbally taunting Samantha by telling her what he was going to do to her. He then raped the victim and choked her to death.

Only twenty feet away, his live-in girlfriend and ten year old daughter were sleeping. They would wake up the following morning and he would join them at the breakfast table. Like turning a switch on-and-off, he spoke of taking his family on a cruise.

"It was apparent that neither his girlfriend or his daughter knew of his crimes," Orange said. "He would tell investigators that 'no one really knew him.'"

Shortly after Keyes' capture in Lufkin, he was then extradited to Alaska to stand trial for Koenig's murder. His trial was set for March 2013 and he was slated to be represented by federal defender Rich Curtner. Keyes was thirty-four years old at the time of his arrest.

Investigation

Israel Keyes was officially extradited to Alaska on March 26, 2012. Shortly after arriving at the Anchorage Correctional Complex, Keyes confessed to the murder of Samantha Koenig, providing information which allowed investigators to locate her dismembered body on April 1st of the same year.

Keyes was initially willing to cooperate with authorities and offered to confess and plead guilty to all charges leveled against him if two terms were met: his trial would last no longer than one year and he would be given the death penalty. He also conditioned his cooperation on the basis that his name and certain details not be released to the media and public.

"I'm not in this for the glory," Keyes told interrogators. "I'm not trying to be on TV. I want my kid to have a chance to grow up. She's in a safe place now, she's not going to see any of this. I want her to have a chance to grow up and not have this hanging over her head."

In June 2012, Keyes attempted to violently escape from a courthouse in Anchorage, in what authorities suspected was a spur-of-the-moment suicide attempt. Keyes was successfully subdued with a taser and taken back into custody alive. Following his attempted escape, Keyes was placed on a suicide watch, which entailed a prohibition on razor blades and sharp objects, regular inspections of his cell, and a 24/7 guard.

The next month, in July 2012, a local news station, WCAX, reported Keyes' connection to the kidnapping and murder of the

Curriers. This lead to Keyes ending all cooperation with the authorities for the next two months.

Modus Operandi

While cooperating with authorities at the Anchorage Correctional Complex, Keyes described his approach to killing thusly: "I would let them come to me... You might not get exactly what you're looking for, there's not much to pick from, so to speak. But there's also no witnesses, there's nobody else around."

Location

Israel Keyes was very methodical in his approach to killing. Unlike most serial killers, Keyes did not kill victims who lived near him. Most serial killers conduct most of their kidnapping and abductions within the vicinity of their home, which leads to an easier investigation and higher chance of being captured. Keyes, on the other hand, was known to take cross-country trips in order to kill.

For example, Keyes killed the Curriers in Vermont while he was living in Washington state. Once he decided to kill, Keyes booked a flight from Washington to Indiana. He then rented a car, removed the battery from his cell phone, and paid for all of his expenses with cash as he drove 1,000 miles to the East Coast. He tested his homemade silencer in New York, retrieved a murder toolkit that he had hidden in Vermont two years earlier, and then identified the Curriers as his next victims. This type of careful planning, attention to detail, and restraint is very uncommon in serial killers.

Victim Profile

Unlike most serial killers, Keyes did not have a specific victim profile. For instance, Ted Bundy, another serial killer who shared many qualities with Keyes, was known to target young, white women between the ages of 15 and 25. However, Keyes had no such victim profile. He alternatively killed or attempted to kill married couples, young woman, men, and several other unknown victims. This allowed him to operate without substantial police scrutiny for some time.

Method of Killing

With the exception of his killing of Bill Currier, Keyes strangled every one of his victims. Furthermore, Bill Currier was shot to death while attempting to escape from the house that Keyes was keeping him and his wife at. Had Bill not been killed in the heat of passion while attempting to escape, it is likely that Keyes eventually would have strangled him to death as well.

Death

After accidentally being provided with razors while on suicide watch, Keyes committed suicide on December 2nd, 2012. He sliced his wrists vertically and hung himself while being held at the Anchorage Correctional Complex. He was pronounced dead immediately.

Prior to committing suicide, Keyes composed a four-page, handwritten letter that was found underneath his body. The letter was covered in blood and was largely illegible, but FBI forensic investigators were able to reconstruct much of his letter.

While the letter did not provide additional details about his crimes and victims, it did offer a glimpse into his psyche and reasons for committing murders. Keyes wrote "Family and friends will shed a few tears, pretend it's off to heaven you go. But the reality is you were just bones and meat, and with your brain died also your soul." Later in his letter he elaborated, "You may have been free, you loved living your lie, fate had its own scheme crushed like a bug, you still die." He repeatedly referred to his victims as a "pretty captive butterfly."

Dr. Stephen Montgomery, a forensic psychiatrist at Vanderbilt University Medical Center analyzed the letter and reached the following conclusion: "It has no remorse, no regard for human life or the victims and that fits with that type of psychopathic personality."

Authorities are still investigating various unsolved disappearances throughout the various states that Keyes visited. It is now believed that he may have targeted homeless shelters where he could kill people who would not be missed.

GWEN HENDRICKS

Gwen Gillespie Hendricks was born into a Navy family in Memphis, Tennessee in 1955.

Her father was a naval officer while her mother was a housewife. Like most military families, they moved often from station to station, according to her father's assignment. Growing up in a devoutly Catholic home and Gwen would embrace the religion with fervor.

Gwen dressed with modesty, wearing button down shirts and minimal make-up. She fostered a nerd look, with wire-rimmed glasses and short hair.

Carrying on the family's military tradition, she joined the Air Force at the age of twenty-five. It was there she would meet Jim Hendricks, twenty-four, who was her instructor.

Jim Hendricks was a tall, strapping Air Force sergeant with an air of authority. He had an easy smile and Gwen found him easy on the eyes.

"Well, it was kind of instant attraction," Gwen recalled. "There was a bit of lust there as he's a very tall, handsome man. The Air Force can tell you that you can't date but they can't tell you who to marry so I went to the Jag office and asked if I could marry my STA and they said 'yes.'"

The two were married in 1980. Jim had a five year old daughter, Season Hendricks, from a previous relationship. In 1982, they would have a son, Ben.

Because of their career choice, the couple spent a lot of time apart during the early years of their marriage. Jim was stationed at Wake Island while Gwen was assigned to Eglin Air Force Base in Florida.

The couple would be reunited in 1986 as Jim was assigned to the Air Force Academy in Colorado Springs. Gwen would not re-enlist in the Air Force, instead taking a job with the Internal Revenue Service.

The couple spent three years in Colorado before Jim would be transferred to Guam in August of 1989. He took the the entire family with him to the island.

"I figured we had a pretty normal family," Season said. "Until we moved to Guam. Things started to change. She (Gwen) would pick fights. She was jealous of the time my Dad and I would spend together."

"She (Gwen) had a different life in mind for herself," forensic psychologist Joyce Smith said. "She was used to having her own money. So when they moved to Guam there was little to do and less money to do it with."

Gwen and the children moved back to the United States, returning to Colorado and leaving Jim in Guam.

She would buy a home in Littleton and once again start working for the IRS. She then joined the junior Chamber of Commerce where she met Terry Knaack and a woman named Rochelle.

"Rochelle was into tarot cards," Gwen said. "And Terry was into new age occultism. My religion, my faith was still very meaningful to me. I wanted to do Bible study with them to get them out of what I considered witchcraft. Rochelle said she wouldn't go to Bible study with me unless I did the cards with her and the same with Terry. So I think I opened up the door to hell. Right after I started, everything went wrong"

During this time, Gwen began to experience health issues. She suffered from dizzy spells and nausea.

Her personality shifted as well, changing from being even-tempered to easily agitated and manic. With her health and ability to focus effected, Gwen stepped down from her revenue collector position to tax examiner.

"Could the illness have played a part in her deciding to kill her husband?" Smith asked. "Maybe. But Gwen was really steeped into religion and sounded like she embraced some of the more fringe elements of Christianity. She truly believed that occultism was a form of witchcraft and that those things could do her harm. So when she suffered from her illness she erroneously attributed it to her dabbling in the occult. She was a woman who preferred supernatural explanations to rational thought."

Gwen also started to grow deeper into debt, buying expensive gifts for friends.

In the fall of 1990, Gwen hired Terry Knaack to help remodel the Littleton home. A few months later, Knaack moved into the couple's basement with the rationale being he would be able to help with the mortgage. With the husband away and a man in the home, Gwen began to fantasize about Terry and starting over with him.

"Terry would talk a lot about wanting to having a ranch for children with special needs," Gwen recalled. "And I started having delusions that he and I would start this ranch together for the children."

"She entered into a fantasy world," Smith said. "She began imagining a life with this other man, having delusions of grandeur of what they would do together. He became her willing accomplice in her dreams, since her own husband was absent because of military duty. So an alternate universe with Terry Knaack became her obsession. What probably started as harmless day dreams soon grew into something sinister."

"I also believe that Gwen had more than a little bit of a Messiah complex. She had this compulsion to save people and it manifested in doling out gifts and handouts to people who she felt were in need. She had this secret life and kept things from Jim who was away on military assignment. Those secrets involved getting into credit card debt."

By January of 1991, Gwen began telling friends that she was having premonitions of Jim dying in a plane crash.

"I had this really bad dream over and over again," Gwen recalled. "Where Jim had died in a plane crash. I was thinking, well after Jim died that I would marry Terry and we'd start this ranch but of course Terry didn't know anything about because it was all in my head."

Gwen then began hearing voices.

"They (the voices) wanted me to sacrifice what was most dear in my life," Gwen recalled. "I remember thinking that I have to answer these voices because this is coming from God. You know, I've got to sacrifice what I loved the most and that was Jim."

Gwen kept a journal where she logged the "premonitions" of her husband's death. She titled the journal "The Courage to Will and Persevere," She described the voices that she heard and believed that God had told her to kill Jim.

"She experienced what we call 'command hallucinations,'" said Smith. "These are sometimes coupled with someone's value system, in this case, it was Gwen's religion. Gwen believed that she should obey God and believed that the voices that she heard were, in fact, coming from God. So this could go bad real quick if those voices told her to do damage to someone."

"She was past the breaking point, a delusional schizophrenic that was not diagnosed. When she confided with friends it was probably with people who shared her same point of view, people who believed in visions, messages from God and premonitions. Gwen was a soft-spoken woman and even if someone thought she was crazy they would not think she would be capable of taking a gun and blowing someone's brains out. She didn't have that violent vibe."

But behind closed doors, Gwen would deal with problems or difficulties in a haphazard fashion. She would often open up the Bible and believed that whatever random verse she came upon was a direct message from God.

"I reread Psalm 90 quite a few times before a small voice said, 'Keep reading, keep reading.'" Gwen wrote in her journal. "After reading the first page of stanzas, I knew I would be protected from the car bombs, the knifings, the guns, the contracts and all the other evil I had seen connected with busting the pornographers and pimps. Those mafia guys play rough, but somehow they just won't be able to get me. Then I turned the page to continue reading. It felt like a giant fist had slammed into my heart. I literally could not breath [sic]. I burst into sobs and sunk to the floor. I cried for Jim because he really was going to die."

Gwen began to prepare for Jim's death, taking out a $300,000 life insurance policy on her husband payable on his death.

She then visited a local banker, informing him that she would be soon be receiving proceeds from insurance claim. Gwen was told that she would not be able to use the money as long as Jim was alive. She then forged a doctor's note which alleged that she had multiple sclerosis. She submitted this note to the Red Cross along with a letter stating that they should be responsible for being her husband back from Guam.

Gwen did not want the proceeds from the insurance for her own material gain. She believed that she could use the proceeds from his life insurance to establish the "James Hendricks Foundation" to aid victims of mafia produced pornography.

"She became obsessed with pornographers," Smith said. "Like most people with Messiah Complexes, she chose an ill of society and focused on that, believing that she was a chosen vessel to help eradicate the 'sin'. In her deluded mind, she needed this money to accommodate God's will to establish this ranch wherein she would save victims of pornography. The only way she could attain this goal would be to kill Jim and take the life insurance proceeds."

"I was very desperate to have him (Jim) back," Gwen said. "I felt like I was at my limit and not really realizing that I actually was really having a breakdown."

With her husband not even dead yet, Gwen began purchasing clothes for herself and the children to wear for his funeral.

She bought silk flowers and boxes of Kleenex for mourning friends and family.

Gwen also increased the amount of Jim's life insurance from $300,000 to $1,000,000.

True to her premonition, she bought a wedding dress for herself and put a wedding ring on layaway for Knaack.

Gwen would ask God to speak to her directly and "guide her hand" as she thumbed through her Bible. When she got to a passage, she would believe that was what God wanted her to study."

"For the first reading, only the last sentence made sense," Gwen wrote. "I had asked if what I felt about Jim's death was real. He said yes.

God can even speak through the dictionary!

After reading the first page of stanzas, I knew I would be protected from car bombs, the knifings, the guns, the contracts and all the other evil I had seen connected with busting pornographers and pimps. Those Mafia guys play rough, but somehow they just won't be able to get me."

"You can see her delusions of grandeur in her journal writings," Smith said. "She had all of the symptoms of a delusional narcissist, truly believing that God made her as the 'Chosen One.'"

Gwen would write that she had a two-way conversation with God about creating the ranch.

"'Oh, so the ranch is in Douglas county near to the Springs so my family will be protected from the mafia guys' Then I knew in Denver, I'm Gwen Hendricks. In the Springs, I'm Gwen Knaack. I had thought the clinic would carry the name of the ranch, but with this new insight, I knew that for safety sake, everything had to be kept separate."

She continued to have health issues as well, as the nausea and attacks of dizziness still had not subsided. Physicians could not determine the cause of her illness. She was eventually diagnosed with Ménière's disease, an ailment that causes vertigo and a fluctuating hearing loss. She had a micro-shunt placed into her ear which only helped relieve the pain she was experiencing.

Her mental health, however, continued to deteriorate.

Jim would return to Colorado for good in May of 1991. It would not be a well-received reunion, however, as the couple fought over everything specifically the living arrangements of Knaack. Jim promptly kicked the boarder out of the home.

He then took control of the finances as he discovered that Gwen had maxed out the credit cards.

"My brother said that she had apparently taken several other credit cards and had maxed them out to the limit," recalled Steve Hendricks, Jim's brother. "And he was furious with her at that point. He did confide in me that he was thinking about leaving Gwen."

Jim would take away all of Gwen's credit cards and this made her extremely angry.

"He took away her power," Smith said. "She got an ego boost by buying expensive gifts for friends and helping out women that she thought were in need. When Jim took that away, she saw him as someone who needed to be eliminated."

Divorce seemed imminent but Gwen seemed immune to it all in her journal writings.

"The funeral, the ranch school, children, the foundation, always being pushed forward," she wrote. "I have to do what I have to do, too. But just for now I'm going to take one day at a time. I'm hoping I don't get too compulsed to do anything more for at least this coming week. I need to rest.

Perhaps I should start by explaining the little voice. It's my voice, but not me. It comes from somewhere inside, and if I don't listen to it, act on it, it becomes a compulsion. If I don't listen and act on the compulsion, it grows stronger and stronger until it dominates all aspects of my life. I learned long ago to listen and do what I'm told. Things work out when I do, and when I don't, things get real miserable...Yes, my little voice is the way God reaches me with the Holy Spirit."

With Jim now home on a permanent basis, The voices in her head grew louder. They began to speak with more urgency in telling her that she had to kill her husband.

"True to her religious background, she did not interpret auditory hallucinations as a sign of mental illness," Smith said. "Gwen was the kind of woman who took the stories in the Bible literally, seeing herself as a modern day Abraham who heard voices from God. You hear it in the way she describes the voices in her head telling her to sacrifice her husband in the same way the Bible speaks of God telling Abraham to sacrifice his son Isaac."

"I said 'Lord I surrender to you,'" Gwen recalled. "I'm hearing voices from God and this is what God wants and I have to get this from God and if this is what God wants then I have to give it to him. So I went out and I bought a gun"

"The voices in her head told her it was time," Smith said. "And true to her value system, she had to obey. For her religion was not a therapeutic aid because of the way she had viewed it. Her God was a vengeful one, a violent one."

On Friday, August 17th, 1991 Gwen drove to Peterson Air Force Base to meet with her husband, a 75 mile drive, to bring him a change of clothes.

"Jim was working late and he asked me to bring him something to eat." Gwen said.

She had informed police that Jim was working all night to prepare for an inspection but changed his mind.

Gwen wrote in her journal about the incident.

When Jim called to say he was on his way home, I went into shock. I knew the time was at hand. I knew I wasn't really ready. I screamed and cried and raged. Then I asked again, if he was meant to die or was I just suckered into some kind of head game. Benjamin's daddy died. I cried myself to sleep that night. I thought what was I supposed to do with two husbands. God has the oddest sense of humor."

"She told me that she was gonna make a nice little picnic for them," Gwen's step-daughter Season recalled. "They were going to make a night of it and that she wanted him to feel good for his inspection."

Gwen left the home and dropped off both Season and son Ben with a friend. When Gwen arrived at the Air Force base, however, she stated that Jim told her that he was heading home. She maintained that the two then went back home in separate cars.

"His truck was in the lead," Gwen said. "I was in the car behind. I remember being so tired, I told him I can't go on anymore. I just want a quick nap and let's get in the back of the truck."

She said that they traveled in separate cars but she became tired and slept through the night at a rest stop along Interstate 25.

Police, however, believed that Gwen lured Jim to an abandoned stretch of highway with the promise of sex.

The two met at the side of the road and Gwen hesitated when thinking of pulling out the gun. She wanted her husband to go peacefully.

"I took the gun out from underneath the seat of the car," Gwen said. "I got into the truck and laid next to him and when I could feel that he was deeply sleeping that's when I shot him."

Gwen would shoot Jim six times.

"It was like I was outside of myself," Gwen said. "Looking and watching what I was doing. I felt very numb, very cold, like I was on auto-pilot. I got back into my car and I took apart the gun and I was just throwing the parts out the window and just driving around, just in a fog, not knowing what I was doing, where I was going. I stopped at a roadside rest stop. Fell asleep. When I woke up and I didn't know everything that happened."

When Gwen arrived back home that Saturday she began making calls to the police, stating that her husband was missing.

On Monday morning, she called Jim's supervisor who sent out two officers to search for him.

One of his co-workers would find his pickup truck on the side of Highway 83 in Douglas County. His body had been placed in the camper shell in back of his truck.

He had been shot six times in the chest and neck with a small caliber handgun.

Gwen would become the primary suspect.

Police noted that she hardly showed any emotion when they informed her of her husband's death.

"Her state of mind was that of a wife with a missing husband," one of the deputies recalled. "When she was telling a story, she couldn't stick with the same story. And that's a clue, obviously, to law enforcement."

Gwen would then break the news to Jim's daughter, Season.

"Gwen said they found him by the side of the road in his car," Season said. "And that he had been murdered. I don't remember her crying. It was the worst moment of my life."

Terry Knaack would be helpful in the case against Gwen. She had been secretly in love with him and given him her diary. He read through her writings and promptly delivered the diary to the Douglas County Sheriff's Department. The sheriffs then instructed him to call Gwen while they would listen in.

Gwen would tell Knaack that she didn't kill Jim but that she wanted to die. Then Douglas County Sheriff's Department Kim Castellano's intuition told her something was wrong. The Hendricks had two pre-teens, a boy and a girl and the boy was never around during questioning.

Castellano believed that Gwen had a problem with males. With one of the male investigators, an Air Force official, by her side, Castellano went back to talk to Gwen.

Once again, the boy was not there. Gwen was overly polite to Castellano, asking her if she wanted anything to eat and jumping up to fix her something before she could answer.

Gwen would totally ignored the male detective.

Castellano used this knowledge to her advantage and befriended Gwen, sensing that the delusional woman would be much more forthcoming with a female officer than a male.

Gwen began trusting her enough that she asked for Castellano's help in balancing her check book. The detective then saw that Hendricks had recently taken out several insurance policies that would be hers when her husband died.

The investigators then used a technique police refer to as the "midnight confession." Castellano and the Air Force official went over to the Hendricks house at eleven at night, waking Gwen up.

Questioning her in the family room, Gwen continued to deny her involvement in her husband's killing. Castellano and her partner then took turns reading from Gwen's journal, tightening the screws on her denial. They also saw Jim's watch on the counter.

Castellano then told her to get dressed and that she was being taken in.

Gwen finally cracked. She curled into a fetal position and confessed.

"Two stories that night—the story of the rest area and the story of Highway 83," she sobbed.

Gwen would go on to describe the highway story.

"There is blood everywhere, I can see it everywhere," she said. "It's terrible. My mind won't let me remember. I don't know if I shot him or not. I don't know what's real anymore."

Gwen was then taken to a local hospital where she stayed for two days for a mental health evaluation. She was arrested upon release and charged with her husband's murder.

After undergoing another mental health examination, Gwen was deemed delusional but understood the charges being levied against her.

Because of this, she was found fit to stand trial.

In court, however, Gwen continued to state that she didn't kill her husband. She said that the body found at the crime scene was not Jim's.

"There was the obvious choice for her attorneys to declare her insane," Smith said. "She had one hell of an imagination and could make things up on the fly. She said during the trial that she became completely convinced that her husband was still alive, going into full blown denial. 'He's still alive, he's out there somewhere and you have to find him', she would say. She was completely delusional."

Her first attorney, Lloyd Boyer, stated that it was physically impossible for Gwen to have murdered Jim Hendricks.

"The lack of gunshot residue inside the Capitol (Jim's car) vehicle," Boyer said. "Indicated that the murder had not occurred in the vehicle. Mr. Hendricks was quite a bit larger than Gwen and she was small, not especially strong and could not have moved the victim into the vehicle."

The investigators failed to produce the gun that Gwen used but the prosecution had another tool at its disposal.

The first link was Jim's watch that they found in Gwen's possession, which showed that she had tampered with the crime scene. The prosecution showed how she was going to use the money from the insurance policies and start a "home for troubled people" that would be near the spot where she killed her husband.

The jury found her guilty of first-degree murder and Hendricks was sentenced to life in prison.

"I just kept my faith that Jim would come rescue me and I would be set free from prison," Gwen said. "Of course, that never happened."

Inside the prison, physicians deemed her to be mentally unfit to be included with the general population and transferred her to the psychiatric unit.

"They got me on anti-psychotics," Gwen said. "And anti-depressants but it wasn't until 1997 that I started having memories of what had happened. At first, it was like just pictures and they hit me like bricks, you know. I killed a great husband and Dad. I robbed Season and Ben of their father. I felt lower than dirt."

She did have help, however, as some legal advocates filed briefs on her behalf, claiming that she had been insane at the time of her trial.

In September of 2000, the Supreme Court of Colorado overturned Gwen's conviction and ordered a new trial.

In April of 2001, a judge ruled that Gwen was not guilty by reason of insanity.

The trial lasted ten minutes.

"She came to terms with what she had done," Smith said. "She had stopped protesting, stop denying and admitted to what she had done."

Gwen was then remanded to a psychiatric care facility in Colorado. She then decided to change her name to "Emi Masai".

"When I lost Jim," Gwen said. "I also lost my children. I longed to be a wife and mother again. I redefined myself as married to Christ and being a mother to all the people I meet."

"By renaming herself she thought that she could obtain a new identity," Smith said. "It was a way of divorcing herself from her past transgressions."

Gwen went through four years of psychiatric treatment where the physicians determined that she was no longer a threat to society. She was released to a residential program where she now helps the needy at Mercy Ministries.

She continues to take her anti-psychotic medication.

"I never want to slip back into mental illness again," Gwen said. "I literally thank God every morning I open my medicine cabinet. I've always said justice wasn't done. Justice in this case would have been my execution. A life for a life. But it's not about fairness. It's about recognizing mental illness and knowing that you're not responsible for what you are doing when you're psychotic."

Gwen has had minimal contact with both her son and step-daughter since she committed the murder of their father.

"I long to see them but they let it be known through family channels that they don't want to see me," Gwen said. "So I respect that."

"I'm really glad that Gwen has helped herself enough to admit what she's done," Season said. "And I hope there never is a time where it gets easy for her to look in the mirror. Because there's never a time where it's easy to be without our Dad."

"I wish I could take it back," Gwen said. "Be a good wife and Mom again. I can't turn the clock back. So all I can do is give them my deepest apology and ask them to forgive me."

WHO KILLED ARLIS PERRY?

DARLA FOSTER

Arlis Kay Perry was a newly married nineteen-year-old when she entered Stanford Memorial Church at Stanford University in the late night hours of October 12th, 1974. She would be found the next morning, the victim of a brutal murder in what appeared to be a ritualistic killing.

Her case has remained unsolved for the past forty-two years. Various rumors and theories abound as to who her murderer was. There is conjecture that she was the victim of the Son of Sam, the Zodiac Killer, the Death Angels and the Process Church.

The police never obtained solid leads on her case and it remains as much a mystery today as it was over forty years ago.

Who killed Arlis Perry?

EARLY LIFE

Arlis was born on February 22nd, 1955 in Linton, North Dakota to Marvin Dykema and Jean Van Beek. She usually wore glasses and had her hair straight. In the lone picture of her available online, her hair is wavy and she is not wearing glasses. This is an unfamiliar look for her and no one knows where or when the picture was taken. She was small, at 5'6" and weighing 110 lbs.

Arlis would graduate from Bismarck High School in 1973 where she was a cheerleader and a member of the Fellowship of Christian Athletes. She had a high school sweetheart, Bruce Perry, and they were both born again Christians. Bruce would be accepted into Stanford University upon graduation while Arlis would stay behind in Bismarck. She remained active in her church as a Sunday school teacher in the Bismarck reformed church.

Then she came into contact with people from the Process Church.

They were six young men that were renting a home across the street from her grandmother. Their names were Father Christian, Brother Thomas, Brother Joseph and three other men who were called "initiates."

The men tried to initiate Arlis into their religion but she soon became disenchanted with their belief system.

She realized that the were devil worshipers.

Arlis then made it a point to try and proselytize anyone who was involved in their church, leading them from Satanism into Christianity.

THE PROCESS CHURCH

The Process Cult became controversial in the early 1970s with its strong ties to the Manson family. Their belief system allowed them to worship both Christ and Satan. The church started in both Los Angeles and New York but branched out to North Dakota, as its leaders wanted the isolation of the hills and woods.

They would have meetings at the Hillside Cemetery in Bismarck and a wooded area behind Mary College. It was here that they would steal the dogs of people who lived in a nearby trailer park and sacrifice them in satanic rituals. People were complaining that they would find their dogs lying dead inside a "majick circle", their bodies badly mutilated.

MOVING TO CALIFORNIA

After graduation, Arlis would continue to participate in the Fellowship of Christian Athletes as a "huddle leader" as well as taking a job as a receptionist in a dental office. She would attend the local junior college for a year as she corresponded with Bruce Perry who was in his first year of studies at Stanford.

Bruce would return home and ask for Arlis' hand in marriage. She would accept and join him as he returned for his second year in Stanford's pre-med program.

Bruce's studies did not leave a lot of time for Arlis and she became a bit restless. She would take a job as a receptionist at a law firm to occupy her time during the day when Bruce would be away, finding work at the law firm Spaeth, Blase, Valentine, and Klein in Palo Alto.

The couple lived at the Quillen House in Escondido Village which was a campus housing unit for married couples.

Arlis got into the habit of taking nightly walks around the campus. Bruce worried for her safety and advised her not to. She stopped the practice until one night she wanted to get out of the home and mail off some letters.

DEADLY CHURCH VISIT

On October 12th, 1974 at around 11: 30 pm, Bruce and Arlis were walking on the Stanford campus. They would discover that the tire on Arlis' car had gone flat. They would have a minor argument as to who was going to take care of it. Bruce went back to the dorm and Arlis would go to the Memorial Church, telling Bruce that she wanted to pray alone.

Arlis entered and several people remembered seeing her. A security guard told her that it was almost midnight and the church was about the close up. She remained inside, however, and witnesses remembered seeing a "sandy-haired man" walk inside.

Arlis didn't return home after several hours and Bruce went out to look for her.

When he didn't find her, he called the police.

The next morning at around 05:45 am, security guard Steve Crawford would discover her body inside the church.

In Maury Terry's book, "Ultimate Evil", he described Perry's murder scene as follows:

"She was found lying on her back, with her body partially under the first pew on the left side of the alcove, a short distance from where she had been seen praying. Above her was a large carving which had been sculptured into the church wall years before. It was an engraving of the cross. The symbolism was explicit.

Arlis's head was facing forward, toward the main altar. Her legs were spread wide apart, and she was nude from the waist down. The legs of her blue jeans were placed upside down across her calves, purposely arranged in that manner. Viewed from above, the resulting pattern of Arlis's legs and the inverted blue jeans took on a diamond-like shape.

Arlis's blouse was torn open, and her arms were folded across her chest. Placed neatly between her breasts was an altar candle. Completing the desecration, another candle, thirty inches long, was jammed into her vagina. She had been beaten and choked. Death was due to her an ice pick being rammed into her skull behind her left ear, the handle protruding grotesquely from her head."

THE AFTERMATH

Security guard Crawford stated that he had locked up the church a little after midnight. He rechecked that the doors were still locked at around 02:00 a.m.

At 03:00 a.m. Perry had called the police and informed them that his wife was missing. The Santa Clara County Sheriff's went to the church and found all of the doors locked. Crawford would return to the church at 05:45 to unlock the doors and he found the west side door open.

The obvious suspect was Bruce Perry and police immediately went to brutally interrogate him.

"You knew your wife was having an affair so you killed her!"

Perry adamantly denied the questions. The police gave him a polygraph test which he passed.

Investigators would found two pieces of identifying evidence from the scene. They were able to collect a DNA sample which was found in semen near the body. The second was a bloody palm print found on one of the candles.

"It's a typical-if there is such a thing-sexual psychopathic slaying," Santa Clara County Undersheriff Tom Rosa said.

Rumors began to circulate around the campus. Some people were saying that Arlis was the victim of a satanist torture rite called the "Black Mass."

Rosa disputed the claim.

"It has no cult-like overtones," Rosa said. "It just happened to occur in a church."

There were no signs of a struggle. The detectives believed that Arlis was the victim of a "fast and sudden attack" as she entered the church around midnight.

Bruce would tell authorities that she often went there to pray when she was having problems.

SON OF SAM

Conspiracy theories would abound as the murder would go unsolved for many years. Some believe that Arlis was not murdered by a lone psychopath but by a satanic cult who stalked her from Bismarck, North Dakota.

Because of the way Arlis' body was positioned (legs spread with a candlestick in her breasts and vagina) people familiar with occult activity assumed that this was a ritualistic killing.

Fueling the speculation was some cryptic correspondence from David Berkowitz.

Berkowitz, the "Son of Sam" killer from New York City, had mentioned the Perry killing as he wrote authorities in North Dakota. He said that he had information on the killer, a man he referred to as "Manson II."

In 1979, five years after the murder, Berkowitz would send police authorities in North Dakota a book. In the margin, he had written: "Arlis Perry, hunted, stalked and slain, followed to California, Stanford Univ."

Berkowitz would claim that he was not the only person involved in the string of New York murders, hinting that he was part of a larger Satanic cult.

Detectives would later interview Berkowitz regarding Perry's murder but realized that he had "nothing of value to offer."

Those following the case, however, believe that Berkowitz should have been interrogated harder.

"Why would he make it up? He had no motive, no reason," crime writer Maury Terry asked. "He's confessed to three murders, he's not getting out."

The "Manson II" Berkowitz referred to was William Mentzer. Mentzer was suspected of being the head of the Son of Sam cult, had ties to the Manson family (although not to Charles Manson himself) and was suspected of being the Zodiac killer.

But was he responsible for killing Arlis Perry?

The answer may lie in the fact that at some point Mentzer was involved in a "hit squad" involving the Process Church. He allegedly performed assassin duties for the higher-ups who needed someone killed.

Interestingly, the serial murders of the Zodiac Killer stopped after Mentzer was in prison There were numerous parallels between the Zodiac Killer and Mentzer. Detectives believe that the Zodiac had military training. Mentzer had served in the Marines during Vietnam and killed ten people. Upon his return from the Vietnam War, the killings began in December of 1968.

The Zodiac would stab two of his victims with a bayonet style knife with rivets. Mentzer had a job where he was making rivets at a local aerospace company.

The Zodiac killer than began taunting the newspapers, sending them a diagram of a bomb while threatening to blow up a school bus. Mentzer later had a job driving a bus. He also had military training in demolition and plastic explosives. One of the survivors said that the killer spoke in a slow monotone with a drawl. Mentzer speaks the same way.

After a final letter to the press, the Zodiac mysteriously vanished in 1974.

Menzer would later be arrested for his role in the brutal murders of Roy Radin in 1983 and a prostitute/madam named June Mincher in 1984.

Radin had been shot more than twenty times in the head. Menzer would then put a stick of dynamite in Radin's mouth and blow off his face.

In the end, however, police didn't believe Menzer had probable cause to be the Zodiac killer and he would never be questioned for the death of Arlis Perry despite the rumors.

Crime writer Terry would investigate Perry's murder on his own and retrace her steps. He thinks that as many as four people were responsible for her death. He believes that the "sandy-haired" man who visited Perry at the law firm was a cult member from Bismarck, someone that she knew from the Process Church.

"She (Arlis) might have heard or seen something she shouldn't have," he said. "They may have feared she would expose them. Someone in Bismarck OK'd this, and someone had the hooks to get help on the West Coast," he said. "This was a pretty sophisticated operation."

BRUCE PERRY

Bruce Perry would complete go on to become a researcher in children's mental health and the neurosciences, becoming an internationally recognized authority in his field.

At Arlis's funeral, one of her law firm co-workers was confused when he saw Bruce. He thought her husband was a different man who had come into the workplace earlier. He witnessed her get into a "heated argument" with the man and assumed it was her husband. The co-worker described this man as "sandy-haired' which would fit the description of the man seen following Arlis into the church the night she was murdered.

Arlis would also note that there were two Bruce Perrys listed in the phone book. There is some speculation that Mentzer pretended to be Bruce Perry and had his name listed in the phone book. People from North Dakota would call and get him instead of Arlis' husband. He would then be able to finagle her whereabouts but subtly asking the family member the right questions.

This is one of the more far-fetched theories. It doesn't seem plausible that Menzer would go to the lengths of putting out a fake name and phone number just to coax Arlis' family and friends to call. Furthermore, he was a black-haired, mustachioed man who did not fit the "sandy-haired" man description.

But what is curious is that Perry's killing would be another instance of a series of unsolved murders that took place in and around the Stanford campus in the early 1970s.

A SERIAL KILLER AT WORK?

The murder of Arlis would be the fourth homicide on the Stanford campus in less than two years as well as the third incident in which the victim was a young woman out alone.

None of the murders were ever solved.

The killings started with Leslie Marie Perlov, a 21-year old Stanford history graduate who worked as a Palo Alto law librarian. She was found strangled to death on February 16th, 1973 in the foothills behind the campus. She had disappeared after leaving her workplace three days earlier.

Perlov's body would be found in a wooded gully where she had a scarf that was "wrapped tightly around her throat." There was no sign of a struggle where her body was found leading authorities to believe she walked there on her own volition.

She was not sexually assaulted but her skirt had been pulled up around her waist and her pantyhose had been stuffed into her mouth. While officers were searching for Perlov, they would find the body of Mark Rosvold, a twenty-five-year-old man out of Palo Alto. Rosvold was believed to have committed suicide the morning after Perlov was murdered. Perlov was last seen near the quarry gate of the Stanford campus, talking to a man with long blonde hair.

Seven months after the Perlov murder, physics student David S. Levine would be found stabbed to death on a walkway just east of the Meyer Undergraduate Library. The attack was estimated to have occurred between 1 and 3 a.m.

An early morning jogger would find the body of Levine. The young man had been stabbed fifteen times in the back and the side.

Like the rest of the murders, there had been no sign of struggle. The detectives believed that the young man was taken by surprise. Levine's empty wallet remained in his pants pocket and they ruled out robbery as a motive for the murder.

Levine was a straight-A student and called brilliant by his fellow students.

San Francisco Mayor Joseph Alioto believed that the murders were the work of a cult called the "Death Angels" who were suspects in the "Zebra" killings in San Francisco. Three months after the murder of Levine, a slaying took place on the UC Berkeley campus that was also rumored to be the work of the "Death Angels."

The Death Angels were a genocidal Black Muslim faction who mostly killed white people from October 1973 to April 1974. They were compromised of four black men: Manuel Moore, Larry Green, Jessie Lee Cooks, J.C.X Simon. The group committed at least 15 murders according to Wikipedia. Author Clark Howard estimates the group to be responsible for as many as two-hundred seventy deaths.

The Death Angeles would use .32 caliber pistols to shoot their victims point blank, however. They would take people by surprise but there were not any instances where they used strangulation or a knife for the initial attack as was the case for Perlov and Levin.

On March 24th, 1974, Janet Ann Taylor was strangled while hitchhiking to her La Honda home after visiting a friend on the Stanford campus. Her body was found early the next morning in a roadside ditch. Taylor was twenty-one years old and the daughter of former Stanford athletic director, Chuck Taylor.

Detectives would later concede that there were "similarities" between the Perlov and Taylor murders.

Both would be strangled although Taylor would be choked by hand instead of a scarf. Neither were sexually violated.

Both were barefoot when their bodies were found and wearing raincoats. Neither of the purses were on the person when their bodies were found.

"We really don't know who we're looking for," Sheriff's Inspector Rudy Siemssen said after the Taylor killing. "We have no motive. She apparently had no money in her purse, although you could speculate that robbery was a motive. It's a rough one."

WHO KILLED THEM?

None of the unsolved Stanford murders seem to be connected in terms of the method of killing. But, on the surface, they all were senseless and without motivation.

In the case of Arlis, there is mere speculation because of her conversations with the Bismarck Process Cult. The rumor is that someone from the cult, a leader or ordered assassin, came out to California because she tried to convert their members to Christ.

What is curious about the case is how the body was positioned. Arlis' pants were moved but placed on top of her body. The pants were positioned legs up, across her calves and her legs were spread apart. Her arms were in a crucifix position and the altar candle was shoved in her vagina.

Looking at her body from above, she was positioned in the Mason's symbol of Freemasonry. So this suggests that her murder was the work of someone involved in the Freemason cult or someone who was trying to make it look as if there was Freemason involvement.

It also appeared that Arlis may have known her killer. Her meeting with the "sandy-haired" man at work or the church may have been a scheduled meeting place. She was a devout Christian woman, used to doing the right thing, so it seems a bit odd that she wouldn't obey the security guard when he told her he was closing up the church.

The speculation is that she was meeting someone, probably the "sandy-haired" man. Who he was or how they came to meet is the question of the day. The problem is that the police failed to see the cult link in the killing, with some kind of warped religious undertones. How much of an evangelist was Arlis and who exactly did she speak with at the Process Cult in Bismarck?

The police were never interested in pursuing that line of thought.

There were rumors in Bismarck that well-known people were part of a satanic cult that performed all kinds of grisly rituals at Pioneer Park and the caves behind the University of Mary. One witness reported that they remembered seeing people come into town in priest's outfits. Only they weren't wearing white collars. They were wearing red collars and upside-down cross necklaces.

Jon Martinson, a former psychology professor at Bismarck State College, doesn't buy the theory that Arlis was stalked from Bismarck to California.

"I remember a lot of weird religious stories going on around here in that time," Martinson said. "Like covens dancing under the full moon and rituals taking place down by the river bottoms. But in her case, I think she was at the wrong place at the wrong time."

After Terry's book "The Ultimate Evil" came out, students around the Bismarck around began trolling around the University of Mary looking for any semblance of satanic cult activity. They found none but it became an urban legend around the town. The caves behind the University of Mary were eventually filled in.

Terry still firmly believes that Berkowitz knew something that the police didn't follow-up on. "It's very important to know that it was Berkowitz himself who raised the connection to (the University of) Mary, and he did it in late 1979 – nearly eight years before The Ultimate Evil was published," Terry said. "Nothing about the Mary

(University of Mary) ties to Arlis' death was made public until the book came out. But Berkowitz knew about cult activities there all along. And I also confirmed that rituals had been occurring there in the 1970s."

Ken Kahn was one of the detectives who flew into Attica State Prison in New York to interview Berkowitz. The Son of Sam killer remained vague and didn't fess up to any details. This led Kahn to believe that Berkowitz was simply messing with the crime writer and knew nothing of the murder of Perry or anyone else at Stanford.

Martinson and Terry remain adamant that Berkowitz knows something as he was documented to have been in nearby Minot Air Force base before he committed his own murders. Martinson showed Berkowitz a series of photographs from people who Terry believed was involved with Perry's murder. Berkowitz identified one of the men in the photo as someone he had met during his satanic cult meetings in Minot.

FOREVER COLD

Detectives were hoping that with advanced DNA technology and handprint databases they would get a lead on the who left behind the semen and bloody handprint.

To date, there are still no leads.

Arlis' parents would stay in contact with the Santa Clara Sheriff's Department for more than thirty years.

Eventually, however, the sheriffs would stop returning their calls.

Arlis Perry's murder remains unsolved.

SISTER MARGARET PAHL

Before the satanic panic of the mid-80s and the accusations of the sexual abuse within the institution, the Catholic Church managed to cover up a murder in Toledo, Ohio. It shouldn't come as a surprise because they were a very powerful organization back in the day and would do anything to save their reputation, including manipulation. The murder victim was a nun, and the only suspect – a priest.

Knowing how the public would react if this got out to the media, the higher-ups from the Catholic Church stopped the investigation completely, removing the accused from the area. However, it took a single letter from 2003 for this case to be re-examined in a new light. And after more than two decades later, the justice was finally served.

Margaret Ann Pahl's early life

Margaret Ann Pahl was born on April 6th, 1909 in a highly religious family. She wanted to become a nurse from an early age, so she studied medicine prior to her decision to become a nun. Margaret joined the Sisters of Mercy when she was only nineteen years old. The Sisters of Mercy is a well-known religious institute created in Ireland, but it quickly spread out throughout the globe. She put her medical knowledge to use and soon became a registered nurse, as well as a nun who dedicated her life to helping those in need.

As the time went by, Sister Margaret Ann Pahl continued her work at the Mercy Hospital in Toledo, Ohio. She was there to consult the younger members of the Sisters of Mercy, and show them the basics. Sister Margaret Ann Pahl was known for her strictness and perfectionism. She didn't hesitate to tell everyone what she really thinks and was very outspoken. Since Mercy Hospital had a chapel, Margaret did her best to keep it in order. She would wake up every morning at 05:00 AM, and start her duties. There were more than twenty nuns at the hospital, and all of them were there to learn from Sister Margaret Ann Pahl.

Besides the nuns, there were also two priests living at the hospital. Their names were Father Gerald Robinson and Father Jerome Swiatecki. They were there to take care of the sick patients and those who are terminally ill. However, Sister Margaret Ann Pahl wasn't keen on Father Gerald Robinson. The two of them quarreled a lot during the time they spent together working at the hospital. As a matter of fact, the majority of the staff, as well as the nuns were familiar with the fact that Margaret Ann Pahl disliked Father Robinson.

Gerald Robinson also came from a religious family, and his mother was the one who made her son become a clergyman. He was born in Toledo, Ohio and stayed in his hometown for the entirety of his life.

His mother financed Gerald's religious schooling from an early age, and he entered the priesthood when he was twenty-six years old. Catholic Church decided to keep him in Toledo to work in a hospital alongside Sister Margaret Ann Pahl. Their personalities simply clashed because Robinson mostly kept to himself, and Sister Margaret thought that he wasn't doing a good job. But he was still loved by the parishioners because he was fluent in Polish and Toledo had a large Eastern European community. So when the two of them got into a fight on April 4th, 1980 because he cut off his sermon early, and Sister Margaret Ann Pahl felt like he owed the parishioners to see it until the end because tomorrow was the Easter Sunday, nobody found it strange or out of the ordinary.

The discovery of the body

It was April 5th, 1980 when one of the nuns opened the doors to the chapel in order to start the early preparations for the Easter Sunday. The hospital expected that the chapel will be completely filled because Easter Sunday is one of the biggest celebrations among Catholics. But as soon as she entered the room, the nun saw a shocking image in front of her. Margaret Ann Pahl's body was laying in the middle of the chapel. The woman was stabbed, and it was clear that something violent has happened during the night. The nun ran outside in a state of panic. She was searching for the phone to call the authorities.

When the investigators arrived at the scene, they were appalled by the viciousness of the murder. The nun was first strangled from behind and then laid down on the floor, where the killer continued to inflict her stab wounds all over her body. The wounds were mostly around her face, on the neck, and torso. However, the killer took the altar cloth and placed it over Sister Margaret Ann's chest before they stabbed her. When the police lifted the cloth off her body, they noticed that the stabs formed an inverted cross. This was a clear indication they were dealing with someone deranged and insane. They weren't sure if the murder had anything to do with Satanism, but everything pointed in that direction. Sister Margaret Ann Pahl also had a bloody cross drawn on her forehead which suggested that the last rite ceremony was performed on her body. In the end, the examiners counted a total of thirty-one stab wounds on Sister Margaret Ann Pahl.

Another detail that was shocking to the investigators was the fact that Margaret Ann's skirt was pulled up, exposing her lower body. The killer also took off her underwear, leaving it around her ankles. However, they couldn't determine if the nun was sexually assaulted because the murder scene looked very clean. It left them wondering if everything was staged to make it appear like the woman was also raped before or after the murder. Since it was the early 1980s and the DNA technology was not fully developed, the investigators had troubles finding any physical evidence on Sister Margaret Ann, or around her body.

The initial investigation

Once they analyzed the scene, the detectives started interviewing everyone in the hospital at the time. They first talked to the nuns who were also deeply disturbed about everything that happened. The majority of them mentioned Father Gerald Robinson and his relationship with Sister Margaret Ann. There were obvious tensions between the two of them, and the nuns thought that he might be involved in a way. However, they weren't sure if he was the killer because he was very withdrawn and quiet. It was hard to imagine that he could hurt anyone.

The entire hospital was searched because the investigators believed that the perpetrator was still there, hiding in plain sight. They went into each room occupied by the nuns and the priests. The detectives found an interesting item in Father Gerald Robinson's accommodation. It was a letter opener that resembled a small dagger. The blade could have been the one which was used to inflict the wounds found on Sister Margaret Ann Pahl's body. Knowing that the two of them argued on the day before the murder, the detectives were fairly certain that they had their suspect. But the letter opener was completely clean, just like the murder scene, and there were no visible traces of blood on it. However, a further analysis showed that there was some DNA material at the bottom of the blade. Unfortunately, it wasn't enough to run the full test in order to determine if it belonged to the murder victim or the killer.

Things were moving fast at the chapel, and the funeral for Sister Margaret Ann Pahl was held on April 8th, 1980. Since Margaret Ann didn't have many relatives in the area, the attendees were the nuns and priests from the hospital. Father Gerald Robinson wasn't officially accused of the killing, and he was not taken into the custody. He was allowed to lead the service for the murdered woman. Father Swiatecki was also there, and he also added a couple of sentences during the funeral.

With only one possible suspect, the police brought Father Gerald Robinson to the police station two weeks after the crime occurred. They wanted to conduct an official interview and hear what he had to say about the night when Sister Margaret Ann was killed. However, before the interview actually started, a monsignor appeared in the police station, and he led Father Robinson out. Soon enough, Father Robinson was transferred from the Mercy Hospital in order to become a pastor. He stayed in the area and was in charge of three parishes in Toledo. He continued to live and work like nothing happened. It was obvious to the detectives who were on this case that something was wrong. But they had no physical evidence that could connect the priest with the murder. And with that, the murder of Sister Margaret Ann Pahl became a cold case.

The cover-ups weren't unusual for the Catholic Church back in the days. They were still very powerful in the 1980s and were capable of hiding their own scandals. If something bad happened within the church, the high-ranking clergymen would intervene almost immediately. They had a developed system that would hide the crimes from the authorities. So the fact that they moved Father Robinson to a different parish wasn't strange at all. This was the best way to conceal the crime and influence the investigators to stop digging deeper. But the 1990s changed everything because the public became familiar with the sexual abuse within the church itself. The witnesses started coming forward, and soon enough, the investigators throughout the United States had more evidence about cold cases that were dormant for decades.

A new witness

The files about the murder of Sister Margaret Ann Pahl laid untouched for a total of twenty-three years. With no new leads or witnesses, the investigators were sure that the case will remain unsolved. It seemed like nobody was willing to talk. But everything changed in 2003 when one witness came forward. As previously mentioned, many women and children started speaking with the authorities about the abuse they suffered from the Catholic priests. An anonymous female sent a letter to Toledo Police Department in 2003. In it, she claimed that she went through a process of recovering her own memories and that she discovered she was a part of the satanic rituals performed by the Catholic priests when she was just a young girl. Since the experience was highly traumatic, her own mind managed to conceal it.

Probably the most interesting part of that letter was that she identified one of the priests involved in the satanic rituals. His name was Father Gerald Robinson. The detectives in Toledo knew the man well. They remembered he was the prime suspect in the murder of Sister Margaret Ann Pahl. The details of that case were very similar to the satanic rituals. After all, the nun was found with the stab wounds that formed an inverted cross. The anonymous woman who sent the letter to the police also mentioned that the priests involved in these rituals performed human sacrifice. Taking everything into the consideration, the investigators decided to open up the case once again in hopes that they missed something which could connect Father Gerald Robinson to the killing of Sister Margaret Ann Pahl.

The woman who sent the letter used the name Survivor Doe to file a civil lawsuit. She claimed that Father Gerald Robinson sexually abused her during the satanic rituals he performed. Survivor Doe said that there were other adults present in the room and she urged them to come out and testify on her behalf. She was unable to identify them on her own because they were wearing nun uniforms and their faces have been covered. Unfortunately, the case itself went nowhere due to the lack of evidence. It was finally dismissed in 2011 and Father Gerald Robinson wasn't charged with the sexual abuse of a minor. But Toledo Police Department started working hard on the case as soon as they received Survivor Doe's letter. New detectives were examining the physical evidence, and they had the technology that would give them better answers.

The re-opening of the case

The arrival of Survivor Doe's letter encouraged the investigators to re-examine the evidence that was collected at the crime scene. This also included the letter opener previously owned by Father Gerald Robinson. The letter opener looked like a small sword or a dagger. Even though the detectives who worked on the case in 1980 suspected that it might be the murder weapon, they never conducted a thorough examination. Toledo Police Department asked for the nun's body to be exhumed, and they sent it to the forensic unit alongside with the letter opener. They determined that one of the facial wounds was very likely inflicted with the letter opener because the blade was an almost perfect fit. However, they couldn't say that the blade was indeed the murder weapon.

After going through the interviews which were conducted immediately after the murder, the detectives noticed that several nuns who were working with Sister Margaret Ann Pahl mentioned that the woman always had a pair of scissors with her. They weren't found in her possession, or anywhere near the murder scene, which led the investigators to believe that the scissors might have been the murder weapon all along. Someone clearly picked them up and hid them from the police. They tested the stab wounds on Sister Margaret Ann's exhumed body and confirmed that scissors might have been the murder weapon as well.

Finally, the forensic unit took the swabs from underneath Sister Margaret Ann's fingernails, as well as from the inside of her underwear. The DNA technology wasn't as advanced in the 1980s but now they could test it in order to find the suspect. Sure enough, the swabs revealed that there was a presence of a male DNA under the nails and in her underwear. But it wasn't a match to Father Gerald Robinson. It belonged to a second person which led the investigators to suspect that there was more than one killer present at the chapel that night.

Since the investigators already had a list of people who were interviewed by the police back in 1980, they decided it might be time to talk to then again. They spoke with everyone they could locate and this led to the discovery of the brand new evidence which wasn't documented more than two decades ago. The police now had witnesses that were able to place Father Gerald Robinson near the crime scene around the time of the murder. It is still unclear why the witnesses failed to mention this detail during the initial investigation, but this allowed the detectives to start building the case against Father Robinson. He was near the chapel when Sister Margaret Ann Pahl was murdered and was in possession of the possible murder weapon.

Then they proceeded to interview Father Robinson himself who willingly went to the police station and gave them his own recollection of the murder. Father Robinson said that he was taking a shower when a nun entered his room in order to inform him that Sister Margaret was found dead in the chapel. He dressed in a hurry and went to the crime scene to see what was happening. When questioned about the murder back in 1980, Father Robinson said something very curious to the investigators. He told them that a man confessed to him that he murdered Sister Margaret Ann, but the priest had no authority to disclose the man's name. However, when asked to confirm this statement in 2004, Father Robinson claimed that he made the story up. Surely, they weren't able to produce a good motive for the murder, but the detectives hoped that Father Robinson would finally start telling the truth about the events that occurred on the night before the Easter Sunday back in 1980.

The arrest and the trial

On April 23rd, 2004 the investigators Tom Ross and Sargent Steve Forrester arrested Father Gerald Robinson for the murder of Sister Margaret Ann Pahl. They picked him up at his home in Toledo, Ohio. He was still working as a priest at the time of his arrest. He pleaded not guilty on May 7th, 2004. Father Robinson was set to wait for the trial out of the jail because his family managed to pay a $400,000 bond. Also, the church placed him on leave which meant that he was not allowed to perform any religious ceremonies during this time. The accusations were shocking to some of the parishioners who knew Father Gerald Robinson for years. As a matter of fact, he gathered a huge following who supported the claims of his innocence. One parishioner called Jack Sparagowski started collecting money that would pay off the defense fees for Father Robinson. He raised a total of $12,000. When asked why he believed in Father Robinson's innocence, Sparagowski told the following: "For someone to commit murder, you have to have a violent streak. I've never heard Father raise his voice or show any expression of anger. The whole thing seems so bizarre."

The investigators working on this cold case were not sure if they should mention the satanic part of the murder. Dave Davison who was the first police officer on the scene stood firm with his beliefs that the whole ritualistic setup of the murder was actually another cover-up which was supposed to steer the investigation into a wrong direction. Prior to the trial, Ross and Forrester invited Dawn Perlmutter who is an expert in ritualistic killings, to hear her own take on the murder. Having in mind that Survivor Doe spoke about satanic rituals in her letter, the prosecution was willing to mention this part during the trial. However, Perlmutter advised them to avoid the narrative because the public is not eager to accept that these things actually do happen and that they might have a hard time convincing the jury.

The trial began on April 17th, 2006 in a Lucas County courtroom. The judge was Thomas Osowik, and he handled numerous high-profile cases in Toledo, Ohio. The media covered the trial thoroughly, and it quickly became one of the most interesting events in Ohio that year. However, there was also some backlash from the public, namely the members of the community who believed that the police was once again covering up the grisly details of the sexual abuse in the Catholic Church. Claudia Vercelloti who is a director of Survivors Network of those Abused by Priests in Toledo, criticized the authorities for focusing their investigation on the murder only. She was positive that there was more to it, and that the sexual abuse described in Survivor Doe's letter needed to be tied in with the killing as well. After all, Survivor Doe named Father Gerald Robinson as one of the abusers. Vercelloti said the following: "We know this is a trial about murder, but the cover-up can't be ignored."

Dean Mandros was appointed as the lead prosecutor, and Chris Anderson was chosen as a part of the team. Both of them were very successful in the past and confident that they could win this case as well, even though they only had circumstantial evidence. Father Robinson found excellent defense layers - Alan Konop and John Thebes. The trial began after the jury selection, and the first to testify was Sister Phyllis Ann Gerold. She was the one who saw Father Gerald Robinson near the scene of the crime at the time the murder was committed. Sister Gerold confirmed that Father Robinson was not in his room and that he was on the floor where the chapel was located.

Even though the prosecution was advised not to mention the ritualistic murders during the trial, they invited Father Jeffrey Grob as one of their witnesses. Father Grob is an expert when it comes to analyzing different rituals. While he avoided connecting the murder to Satanism, he did mention that a priest would have enough knowledge to stage the murder scene and make it appear like a ritual was performed on the body of the victim. He wasn't able to confirm that

Sister Margaret Ann Pahl was killed during the ritual itself, but Father Grob said that an inverted cross was a very common symbol in Satanism.

The prosecution managed to recruit a famous forensic investigator Dr. Henry Lee who was a part of several prominent cases including the murder of JonBenet Ramsey and the O.J. Simpson trial. Dr. Henry Lee was there to give his assessment of the possible murder weapon, as well as to determine if the crime scene was staged. While he confirmed that the letter opener which was found in Father Robinson's possession could have been the blade which was used to kill Sister Margaret Ann Pahl, he was uncertain about the imprints on the altar cloth. One bloody trace was very similar to the decorations found on the handle of the letter opener. Dr. Henry Lee could not dismiss the claims that the murder scene was staged in order to look like a sexual assault, as well as a satanic ritual.

The defense called Dr. Kathy Reichs, a well-known forensic anthropologist to give her own evaluations of the wounds found on Sister Margaret Ann Pahl's exhumed body. Dr. Reichs said that the findings were inconclusive and she suspected that another weapon was used to kill Sister Pahl. However, she couldn't rule out the possibility either. Dr. Reichs mentioned that the scissors owned by Sister Margaret Ann Pahl were a more believable murder weapon. She came to this conclusion after examining the images of the stab wounds provided to her by the defense.

Father Gerald Robinson stayed silent during the trial. He never spoke to anyone and refused to testify on his behalf. His defense lawyers argued that the prosecution had no physical evidence tying their defendant to the murder. Everything they presented was circumstantial, including the letter opener. Not to forget that an unknown male DNA was discovered at the scene as well. The defense also stated that Father Robinson didn't have any motive for the murder which sparked a heated discussion about the fact that Father Robinson argued with Sister Pahl one day before the killing.

The verdict and aftermath

The jury retreated to discuss the case on May 11th, 2006. It took them only six hours of deliberation to reach the verdict. Father Robinson sat in the courtroom, wearing his clerical collar, looking calm and composed. The jury found him guilty of the murder of Sister Margaret Ann Pahl. The judge sentenced him to fifteen years to life, with the possibility of a parole after ten and a half years. Father Robinson refused to comment on the ruling, not breaking his silence throughout the whole procedure. He was escorted to Lucas County jail.

As the prosecution exited the courtroom, they were cheered by the people waiting for the sentencing. Dean Mandros, the lead prosecutor made a comment immediately after leaving the court in which he said: "I don't see it as a reason to celebrate. We're dealing with a homicide case. We're trying to hold the person responsible accountable. We didn't go back in the office and high-five each other." Mandros also mentioned that he was certain Father Robinson murdered Sister Margaret Ann Pahl in a fit of blind rage. When asked about the ritualistic part of the murder, he dismissed it. Instead, Mandros said: "Perhaps the most common scenario there is for a homicide: A man got very angry at a woman and the woman died. The only thing different is that the man wore a white collar and the woman wore a habit."

Father Gerald Robinson suffered a heart attack in May of 2014. He died on July 4th, 2014 in Franklin Medical Center in Columbus, Ohio where he was imprisoned. Father Robinson became a first known Catholic priest in the United States who was found guilty of murdering a nun.

THE MURDER OF MICHELE AVILA

AIMEE BARNES

Michele Yvette Avila, known as Missy to her friends and family, was born in Los Angeles California in 1968. She grew up 20 miles north of L.A. in Arleta with her mother Irene and three brothers; Ernie, Mark, and Chris. She was the focus of two books, a movie starring Patty Duke as her mother, and several TV shows. However, it was not her life that was remarkable but rather her death. At the tender age of 17, just as her life was beginning, she was murdered.

As horrible as any murder is, this one was made more heinous by the fact that Missy was murdered by those she trusted most, her best friends. The same girls whom she had grown up with on their quiet street in Arleta. Girls she had trusted implicitly with her deepest secrets. That is why the story of Missy's murder must start years before it happens when she was just eight years old when the new girl moved with her family into the house right around the corner from her own.

Karen Severson was that new girl and Missy was the first to befriend her.

Shy, awkward Karen moved into the house right around the corner from the Avila house. Missy invited Karen to her home to play dolls and the two became fast friends. They could often be seen walking arm-in-arm to school or jumping rope and sharing secrets under the willow tree in the Avila front yard.

"Then at 11:30 I went to my friends house. We played barbies, then we went swimming. After we had gone swimming, we played barbies again. Then we went swimming for a long time. (My friends name is Karen.)" This quote from Missy's diary on August 31, 1978 is typical of the other entries surrounding it. In fact, throughout the pages shared by Shavaun Avila, Missy's sister-in-law, Karen is mentioned in the same way on all but one page.

While Laura Doyle had been Missy's friend since long before Karen moved in, she was never as close to Missy as Karen had become. Karen often involved herself in anything Missy and Laura were doing. She seemed jealous of the friendship.

In junior high, both girls fell in with a drinking, drugging crowd of kids. Mark Avila, one of Missy's brothers, was quoted by the Los Angeles Times as saying, "She fell in with a bad crowd. She had to have low self-esteem to hang around with people like that."

By the time Missy and Karen reached 10th grade, events had begun to divide them. While Missy blossomed into a green-eyed beauty, Karen gained weight and began her long relationship with the green-eyed monster. It was that very jealousy which led to the sundering of the friendship and eventually to Missy's death.

Karen craved the attention Missy received. More than one person was quoted saying Karen was obsessed with Missy and wanted to be her. However, Missy was the complete opposite of Karen. Missy was outgoing, popular, and pretty. Karen was overweight, shy, and would have been completely unknown to fellow students if not for Missy. This just made Karen angrier. She blamed Missy for her lack of popularity and began trying to sabotage Missy's.

In one incident, Missy was beaten up by a group of girls who believed a rumor that she had slept with their boyfriends. One of the girls told Missy shortly after the attack that it had been Karen who started the rumor. Still fiercely loyal to her friend, Missy refused to believe that Karen would do that. "Missy was so mad at the girl for telling her it was Karen's fault. Missy 'knew' Karen would never do anything like that." Irene Avila would later say. "Missy made great lasagna, dreamed of becoming a physical therapist, and was fiercely loyal to her childhood friends."

In her junior year, Missy dated a boy named Randy. After a month, she broke up with him because he liked to drink and do drugs too much. He soon started dating Karen and they moved into an apartment together. This soon became party central despite the fact that Karen had given birth to a baby girl she named Stephanie after her sister and that infant was present. Missy told her mother of an incident where Randy pulled her onto his lap just as Karen walked in. Missy quickly got up and told Randy she wasn't interested in dating him again. She suggested Karen leave him. "Karen was really upset because the guy she wanted didn't want her," recalls Irene. "He wanted Missy."

In a similar incident, Laura Doyle's boyfriend, Victor Amaya, had broken up with her due to her constant jealousy. "I broke off the relationship because she was jealous of me talking to other girls, including Missy. Laura refused to accept the breakup and became bitter." Victor would later say.

One day, Laura's drives by Victor's while he and Missy are holding hands and kissing at the end of his driveway. Enraged, she pulls down her window to tell them that they were caught and call Missy names like 'slut' and 'whore.' Instead of apologizing and denying any feelings for Missy as Laura had expected him to, Victor tells her to go away. "We (he and Missy) argued with Laura at my house in Arleta. Me, my brother Noah and Missy had been standing in front of the house when Laura drove up. Laura wanted to know 'Why is Missy here?' and I ordered Laura to leave. Before she drove away she said 'I'm going to kill that bitch!' I didn't take the threat seriously and I never reported it to police."

By September 1985, both Karen and Laura had stopped speaking to Missy. She was divested by the loss of her two closest friends. On September 21st, Karen sees Missy at a local park and attacks her with a beer bottle. She slaps and pushes her former confidant before friends break up the fight. Missy's mother heard of the confrontation but did not later connect it to her daughter's murder. After all, the girls had often quarreled during their long friendship.

"Her only problem, at least on that fateful day was that she was very popular with the boys and this drove Laura Doyle and Karen Severson crazy." Deputy District Attorney Tamia Hope said at the trial. "They started out yelling at her, telling her how mad they were at her, and how she slept with entirely too many boys and messed up entirely too many relationships."

Shortly after that confrontation, the girls apologize to Missy and make up. According to her mother, her excitement was easily noticeable. She is thrilled to have her two best friends back in her life.

On October 2nd, Missy told her mother she was going out with Laura. "When Laura got to the house, the girls were laughing and talking about boys. As they drove off they seemed very carefree. I remember how especially pretty Missy looked that day. She was all excited to go. She even turned to me and said "I love you" which is something she did not ordinarily do. That scene haunts me even today."

They met up with Karen and her roommate Eva Chirumbolo at Stonehurst Park in Sun Valley. From there they drove in two separate cars to Wicky up, also known as Colby Canyon. A spot all three girls were familiar with as it was a popular party spot for teens. A campground in the Angeles State Forest a 45 minute drive from Arleta.

"Karen said that she and Laura 'planned to scare Avila.' I didn't know what they had planned. I didn't know how far this was going to go." Eva would later say at Laura and Karen's trail.

What happened next is pieced together by the three girls testimony. When they reach the forest, they park in a dirt lot near a wooded area near the creek. Laura and Karen get out of their vehicles and begin yelling at Missy who is still sitting in Laura's car. Missy begins crying and the girls force her out of the car and begin pushing her around calling her names and accusing her of stealing their boyfriends.

Eva says she decided to get out of the vehicle as by this point the confrontation was becoming increasingly intense. Missy, who had just been laughing and listening to music with who she believed were her best friends was not crying and noticeably shaking with fear. Laura grabs her wrist and forcibly pulls her towards a trail into the wooded area. Missy resists until Karen comes up and pushes her.

"All four of us walked down an embankment to the creek. Laura and Karen continued screaming at Missy," says Eva, the prosecution's star witness. She continues her retelling of that fateful night's events by saying Laura yanks Missy by her hair and accuses her of sleeping with Victor. She steps up to the creek and pushes Missy towards Karen who shoves her to the ground.

Missy is frantic and begs for forgiveness and frantically pleads for her life. At this point, Eva says she became terrified of what was to come and runs back to the car. "I was scared so I ran back to where the cars were parked," says Eva. She hears Missy scream for her to help her but she feels helpless and feared for her own life. Unlike the obese Karen and aggressive Laura, both Missy and Eva are petite and no physical match for either girl let alone both of them at once.

Karen and Laura continue to beat and batter Missy. One of her earrings is ripped from her ear and becomes tangled in her hair. Her beautiful waist length hair is hacked at with some sharp instrument and clumps of it litter the ground. Laura shouts, "You're going to pay for what you've done! You're going to pay for sleeping with our boyfriends!"

They carry the 98 pound Missy, as she struggled to escape, down to the shallow water, a mere 8 inches deep. As she continues to struggle they forcefully hold her head under the water. They continued to hold her head underwater for several minutes after she quit struggling and then carry a 4-foot, 100 pound log over and put it on her neck to keep her head under the water.

Still scared, Eva asked Laura several times, "What happened? Where's Missy?" She was told that she was drowned. She testified that while both Laura and Karen appeared jittery after the murder but they weren't sorry they had done it. "A few minutes later, Karen and Laura joined me. Karen Severson jumped into her car and drove away. When I got into the car with Laura, she said 'We killed Missy.' Then she said, 'Missy deserved to die because she slept with Victor.'"

Four hours after the murder, Laura called the Avila house and asked to speak with Missy. Irene was confused. "I told her I thought Missy was with her," she says. Laura informed her that she'd dropped Missy off to talk with three boys in a blue Camaro while she went to get gas. When she came back, Missy and the boys were gone.

Three days later, on October 5th, hikers found Missy's body right where the girls had left her, face down in the creek with a log anchoring her in the water. One of the first policemen on the scene said, "The young woman's body was a terrifying sight." Her face was badly beaten and her hair was chopped off.

When the police came to inform Irene Avila that they had found Missy, she collapsed. At the funeral, she collapsed again and had to be rushed to the hospital by ambulance. The grisly murder of her only daughter was simply too much for Irene to bear. Both Karen and Laura attended the funeral of their 'best friend.' Eva Chirumbolo did not.

Shortly after the funeral, Karen and her 2-year-old daughter moved in with Irene. Karen vowed to find the 'animal' that murdered her friend and 'helped' Irene track down clues. She lived with Irene for three months sitting up nights sharing memories of Missy. Irene Avila said, "She was close to me, like another daughter. Karen was my daughter's best friend. They grew up together."

Karen was obsessed with the murder. She visited Missy's grave two or three times a week, often leaving balloons or flowers. The walls of her bedroom with pictures of her dead friend and newspaper articles about her murder. Worse, she began frequently visiting the scene of the murder and was seen sitting by the creek drinking beer.

The cover up began falling apart when Karen announced out of the blue that Laura wanted to change her story. Karen then summoned Laura to Irene's house where she told Missy's mother that she had lied. There was never any blue Camaro or any boys. She now claimed that the truth was she had dropped Missy off near a L.A. church to deliver $500 to a drug dealer.

Not long after that Karen claimed that Missy was haunting her. She claimed to see her sitting on the Avila's couch, floating over her while she slept, and even keeping her car from starting while visiting Missy's grave.

The mystery of who murdered Missy Avila might have never been solved if it weren't for the suicide of Eva Chirumbolo's brother which made her understand the loss the Avila family felt. She finally came forward in July of 1988 and told police everything. She was not charged as an accessory to murder in exchange for her full cooperation.

Based on her recounting of the events, Karen Severson and Laura Doyle were arrested and charged with 1st degree murder. Their trial date was set for September 18, 1989. Both women plead 'not guilty' and Karen told officers, "I know the details of what happened to Missy but I'm not going to say."

Irene's grief is worsened by the shock of having intimately shared it with the woman who caused it. "She was Missy's best friend," says Irene, "but she was jealous of Missy's family, Missy's looks, Missy's popularity and even Missy's relationship with me." Missy's brother Mark, 24, agrees. "Karen, wanted to be Missy," he said to People.

Yet if Karen had been full of love and hate, jealousy and guilt, she kept it hidden. "We talked to Karen several times during the investigation," says L.A. Deputy Sheriff Bill Patterson, "and not once—I mean never—did we suspect she was in on the murder."

"When they told me that it was Karen and Laura, I didn't believe the cops," Avila said. "I couldn't believe it. I couldn't believe it."

Irene never suspected Karen either, it was beyond her comprehension that someone so close to Missy could have been involved in the killing. "Who knows, maybe Missy was haunting Karen to make her pay for what she did," says Irene. "If it's possible, then I hope to God she's haunting her each night in prison."

On January 31, 1990 both Laura Doyle and Karen Severson, both now 22, were convicted of 2nd degree murder. The prosecutor pushed hard for a 1st degree murder conviction saying, "Our position was that this crime was a deliberate, well-planned torture and execution of Missy, and needed to be treated as such," one prosecutor told the Daily News 11 years ago, after Doyle's parole was denied. However, several jurors said afterwards that they and not been convinced that the murder was planned in advance rather than a crime of passion.

Both women received 15 years to life. Karen served her time at the California Institution for Women in Corona, California. Laura, however, was sent to Valley State Prison for Women in Chowchilla, California.

They first became eligible for parole in 1997. During parole hearings, Karen admits she arranged the walk in the woods but says she only planned to torment Missy. Laura also becomes more forthright at her parole hearings and in 2002 she admits to coaxing Missy into the water and killing her but insists that Karen was the ringleader.

During her incarceration, Karen is described as the modal inmate. She was active in self-help groups, Bible studies, tutoring fellow inmates, and earned a Bachelor of Arts degree in psychology and a doctorate in theology. She was also diagnosed with Multiple Sclerosis during her time in prison.

On July 8, 2011, the parole board recommended Karen Severson's release despite the Avila family's objections. Irene Avila was not able to attend this parole hearing for health reasons. After a 2001 parole hearing for Karen, Irene suffered a heart attack and was ordered by her doctors to never attend another one.

Karen's parole was subject to a four month board review period and then the governor has a chance to intervene. While prosecutors say their hands are tied, the Avila family held out hope and began collecting letters opposing her release to send to Governor Brown.

None of their attempts were successful however, and Karen was release on parole. Upon hearing of Severson's release, Irene Avila said, "I wish that girl would die. I feel bad for my sons. I feel bad for everybody who knew her. This was a terrible injustice, a terrible injustice. I don't understand why people who commit murder, they let 'em out." Laura Doyle was paroled shortly after Karen Severson.

The wounds of loss were ripped wide open with the release of Missy's murders. "I hate her. I hate her. I hate her," said Irene Avila, now 72 upon hearing of Laura Doyle's release. "Both should have suffered the death penalty. They are free. My daughter is in the ground."

One would think the story ends there, but it does not.

Despite public outcry, Karen Severson wrote a memoir about the case entitled "My Life, I Lived It." In the memoir, she recounts explicit details of the murder. When asked about the memoir, Karen said, "I walked away. They don't have a daughter. They don't have a sister. I don't have a friend."

When told that there were several other ways she could make money, Karen said, "Like what, sell myself?" Severson told those who questioned the morality of her making money off of her crime that she would donate a portion of the proceeds to an anti-bullying group.

When asked why she does not donate all of the proceeds, Severson responded, "I didn't say everything. I have to live. It's hard to get a job out there."

Unfortunately the 1st Amendment says criminals cannot be prevented from telling their stories. However, the Avila family filed a wrongful death civil lawsuit against Severson and the book's distributor for slander and infliction of emotional distress.

"Today we're filing a lawsuit against a vicious killer who has been profiting off her crime," Shavaun Avila, Missy's sister-in-law told news sources outside court. "It's not about us making money off this lawsuit, it's about letting the public know that crime is paying in California."

In addition to the civil lawsuit, the Avila family pushed legislation in the state assembly called "Missy's Law." It's intended to help family members of crime victims recoup money from a perpetrator who has made money from a book or movie deal based on their crime. The bill was sponsored by State Assembly member Nora Campos.

"This law should have been passed a long time ago," Irene Avila said. "It's like they're giving them a reward for killing somebody."

In response to public outcry and the pending lawsuits, the distributor of Karen Severson's book changed the price to zero, ensuring she would never profit from it.

On October 15th, 2015 Governor Jerry Brown of California passed Missy's Law. The family celebrated it as a huge victory. "I feel like we've won a really big battle, but there's still a war going on out there, and we're going to keep battling as long as it takes," said Shavaun Avila.

For her part, Irene Avila has this to say, "All I can say is, 'Girls, watch out whom you trust.'"

SPREE KILL : THE TRUE STORY OF GEORGE BANKS

ANA BENSON

Spree killers are a special kind of murderers who are completely different from serial killers. They commit two or more murders in a short period of time. This means that they do not experience the cooling-off period which is typical for a serial killer. As a matter of fact, their killing spree is often quick and pretty violent.

Driven by an uncontrollable rage, spree killers would often turn on their families, co-workers, or any group of people that wrong them in any way. What triggers these crimes? The debate is still ongoing but it is usually connected with a major event in a killer's life such as a breakup or an argument with someone who is more superior to them.

So when George Banks, a former prison guard, began his rampage in Jenkins Township, Pennsylvania, the entire police force went out to hunt him and try to prevent his further unraveling. Unsure what started his killing spree, they weren't ready for the crime scenes he left behind. They knew he had military training since he worked at a prison and that catching him would be a problem. The law enforcement also realized that they are dealing with a highly psychotic individual that simply had nothing to lose.

So what exactly happened on that autumn day in 1982 and why did George Banks turn on those who were closest to him?

Early life

George Banks was born on 22nd of June, 1942 in Wilkes-Barre, Pennsylvania. He was a mixed race due to the fact that his father, John Mack was African American, while his mother Mary Yelland, was Caucasian. His parents were not married and he was born out of wedlock which was not well received back in that time. Since George Banks was multiracial, his childhood was particularly rough and he was often bullied by his peers. The abuse would be focused on his racial background but it did sometimes involve the lack of a father figure in his life.

He was quite smart but George Banks didn't excel in school. Banks attended St. Mary's Catholic School. He was simply unable to express himself properly so he would get bad grades as a result. It was clear that he will not be going to a college after the high school so he chooses a different path. George Banks made a decision to enroll in the Army 1959. Banks was unable to control his temper back then which led to numerous fights and disputes with both fellow soldiers and his superiors. He didn't care about a rank and would often argue with the officers. He was discharged from the army in 1961. Disappointed with his life so far, Banks decided to stop being an upstanding citizen and get involved with crime.

Banks was only nineteen when he and his gang entered Brazil and Roche tavern with an intention to rob the cash register and take everything they could find of value. The owner of the tavern happened to be inside because he was cleaning up the bar and he didn't have any weapon to defend himself with. After noticing the owner, George Banks aimed his gun and shot him. The owner didn't die but he was badly injured. Banks was arrested shortly afterward. The sentence was six to fifteen years in a State Correctional Institution. He spent eight years in Graterford prison but was paroled in 1969.

After the time he spent behind the bars, George Banks wanted to live his life to the fullest so he married his friend Doris Jones as soon as he got released from the prison. He was set on changing his ways and starting a family was the first step. The marriage lasted for seven years and the couple welcomed two daughters. However, George did physically abuse Doris Jones and their fights often got pretty violent. Banks was unfaithful to her and had many lovers during the time they were married. Doris simply couldn't take it anymore but surprisingly she wasn't the one who filed for a divorce. As a matter of fact, Banks did so in 1976. When the paperwork was completed, Banks felt like a free man. He wanted to go out and date other women without the weight of a marriage on his shoulders.

He preferred Caucasian women after his separation from Doris Jones and he did have one long-term relationship with a woman called Sharon Mazillo. But he was still a cheater and would often have more than one lover on the side. He purchased a house in Wilkes-Barre and began making his own little harem. He had four girlfriends living with him at one point. Banks had at least one child with each and every lover. It seemed that this kind of lifestyle didn't bother the women so they continued to live with Banks for years.

Banks' house was located in a white neighborhood and he claimed that the relations between him and the people who lived on the same street were very intense. The fact that he was African-American was apparently a huge problem. His neighbors didn't agree with his group of lovers either. Banks' children were also the targets of racial hatred according to him. He would later comment on that by saying: "They attempted to burn my house, smashed several windows, squirted my babies with water when they were in the yard and intimidated the girls and children."

On the other hand, his former neighbors told the authorities that Banks and his family mostly kept to themselves. They refused to communicate with the families who lived nearby and Banks would always scold both his girlfriends and children for talking to them. Banks didn't want them to socialize and he controlled their movement.

In 1980, Banks got employed by State Correctional Institute Camp Hill. It was also located in Pennsylvania. He got accepted to the position of a watchtower guard. Somehow his criminal records were overlooked and George Banks became a figure of authority, working on the side of the law this time. But after a couple of months, the changes in his behavior were more than obvious. He was a bit obsessed with famous cult leaders such as Charles Manson and Jim Jones. Banks would also start reading various survivalist publications back then and it looked like he was preparing for some type of racial war.

He started his mental downfall in 1982 and talked excessively about the previously mentioned racial war. He shared his thoughts with the fellow prison guards who would later testify that Banks told them that the conflict will not be avoided and that he wanted to spare his mixed race children from the possible hate they would experience in the process. He wanted to shield them from the hatred he felt when he was younger.

George Banks received a suspension from his work in September of 1982 because he got into a fight with his boss. His treats also involved suicide and he locked himself in a guard tower saying that he would take his own life. The colleagues intervened and they managed to calm Banks down. The whole situation was unusual because it appeared that Banks experienced a full mental breakdown. He was put on a leave of absence until he recovers.

Banks was asked to visit a psychiatrist in a local hospital who might help him with his problems. He ignored the recommendation and the possible help he could have gotten from the doctors. Banks continued his downward spiral into psychosis and started obsessively thinking about killing his girlfriends and children. His paranoid thoughts about the racial war consumed him on a daily basis. Unfortunately, the tragedy was just a couple of weeks away and even though there were plenty of warning signs, nobody prevented it.

Schoolhouse Lane murders

The evening of 24th September 1982 didn't seem even a bit out of the ordinary in Banks household which was located on 28 Schoolhouse Lane. George consumed large quantities of alcohol and prescription pills. He felt powerless over the fact that he was suspended from his job a couple of weeks ago. Plus, his ex-girlfriend Sharon Mazzillo didn't want to give him the full custody of their son, Kissamayu Banks. George was the primary caregiver but Sharon didn't let him take the child into his home so he was living with the mother at a trailer park. After a couple of hours, he closed the door to his bedroom and went to sleep.

Banks woke up early the next morning, took his AR-15 semi-automatic rifle which was by his bed and entered the living room. Regina Clemens, Susan Yuhas, and Dorothy Lyons who were Banks' girlfriends were sitting on the couch, talking with each other. He raised and pointed his rifle, shooting Regina first. The bullet went through her head. Remaining two women were clearly in shock and disbelief because neither of them even tried to run and hide from Banks. Instead, they continued to sit down, staring at Banks.

George Banks then shot Susan five times. The bullets hit her stomach and abdomen. Dorothy was next and she had three bullet wounds on her arms, neck, and torso. The wounds indicated that she tried shielding her face from the attack. Banks moved on to find his children, who were in a nearby room. He shot his twenty months old daughter Mauritania once in the head. Boende who was four years old was killed in the same way.

The rest of Banks' children were upstairs sleeping so he climbed the stairs and found six years old Montanzima in her bed. She received a gunshot to her chest and didn't even wake up when Banks entered the room. Nancy Lyons who wasn't Banks' daughter slept in the bed beside

Montanzima. She was shot twice in her arm and chest. Foraroude was Banks' final victim on Schoolhouse Lane and he was just one year old. Banks placed his rifle on the back of the boy's neck and delivered the fatal shot.

Even though George Banks murdered his entire family that was present at the house, he still had some unfinished business. He went into his bedroom and changed his bloody clothes. Banks selected military fatigues and a T-shirt that had a chilling sentence on the front – Kill em all and let God sort them out. His killing spree did not end there because he had another location to visit.

He exited the house in a hurry and bumped into Jimmy Olsen and Raymond Hall Jr. They were just leaving their home which was on the other side of the street but Banks though of them as possible witnesses who would call the authorities and have him turned in. He had the rifle in his hand and since both of them already saw him, made a decision to shoot the men. Both Olsen and Hall were hit in the chest. Hall died on the spot but Olson did manage to get to the hospital in time and survive the attack because his gunshot wounds weren't life threatening.

Heather Highlands Mobile Home Park murders

Sharon Mazzillo moved into Heather Highlands Mobile Home Park after her breakup with George Banks. She lived there with their son Kissamayu and her mother would often come by in order to help with the child. George Banks drove straight to the mobile home park and burst through the door. He shot Sharon in the chest as soon as she saw her, leaving no time for an argument. Sharon's mother run to the phone as George made his way to his son's room.

Kissamayu was sleeping and he placed the barrel on his son's forehead. The fatal shot was delivered only a couple of seconds later. He returned to the living quarters where Sharon's mother was attempting to call for help and fired the rifle into her head. He then noticed Sharon's nephew Scott who was staying with them that morning. Scott was crying and was upset after witnessing the murders. George didn't hesitate for a moment, hit the boy with his rifle and continued to scream saying that the boy was bullying Kissamayu because he was half African-American. He then shot him in his head, right behind the boy's ear.

George Banks exited the trailer but he didn't notice Sharon's brother who was hiding in the closet during the entire incident. He found the phone and called the authorities who arrived soon after. Since he was familiar with the lawsuit and knew who George Banks was, Sharon's brother told the police everything he knew about the crime, including the name of the killer.

The police have already found Olsen and Hall back on Schoolhouse Lane and connected Banks to those shootings as well because they knew he was one of the neighbors living on that street. There was no need to hesitate anymore so they entered Banks' home. The police officers who were on the scene were shocked to discover a total of nine bodies inside the house. The house looked like something out of a horror movie and the only living thing inside was the family's dog who was constantly barking. Now they were sure that the killer was extremely dangerous and that they need to find him as soon as possible.

Banks drove away and made a decision to ditch his own car. He stole another vehicle and searched for a place to rest. He finally settled for a secluded parking lot, exited the car and lay down in tall grass. George Banks slept for a couple of hours undisturbed and went straight to his mother's house after he woke up. He told her what he had done and she was in disbelief. Banks' mother called his house in order to check if he was telling the truth or not. The police answered the phone and Banks started talking to them after a couple of minutes.

The police wanted to know more about the crime but they also needed to locate him because they feared he might continue his killing spree. Banks realized what they were doing so he quickly hang up the phone. He gathered up his things, found more bullets for his rifle and drove off to an abandoned house in a less populated area. His friend used to live there so he knew that no one was currently residing there. In the meantime, the law enforcement reached his mother's house and talked to the woman herself. She told them everything she knew, including Banks' current location.

Banks was completely surrounded in the abandoned house by over one hundred officers and the police tried to make him surrender. His mother was driven there by the law enforcement as well, negotiating with Banks. Since they knew he was well armed, they attempted to make him come out by saying that his children did survive the shootings and that they needed his own blood for transfusion. Nothing worked and the police stood outside for hours, wrecking their brains about possible strategies that would make Banks surrender.

They contacted Robert Brunson who was Banks' best friend and a fellow prison guard. He talked to him and finally made Banks exit the house with his hands in the air. The standoff was over without any additional shootings. Banks was taken straight to the police station and received various charges which included eight first degree murders, theft, robbery, assault, and attempted murder.

Chief Detective Jim Zardecki who was at the scene that day would later say: "I looked at him, handcuffed to a chair and I felt like a balloon that had suddenly been pricked. I started to quiver. My eyes watered. I thought, what really happened here? My God, what happened? Until then, we'd been reacting. We hadn't time to think about it. We were more lucky than good. He could have blown anybody away."

The investigation and the trial

Once George Banks was in the custody, the detectives started talking with him in order to discover what exactly happened and why he snapped. He immediately told them that he would have committed suicide in the empty house if he knew that his children were dead. Even though he didn't want to give any details about the killings, he didn't deny that he was the perpetrator.

Banks didn't provide the investigators with plenty of details but they did have his mother's confirmation that he did, in fact, confess to her. There was no doubt that George Banks murdered his girlfriends and their children. However, his psychosis started to show at this point and Banks started talking about the conspiracy. Banks believed that the police officers were involved in murdering his wounded children.

Banks' trial was scheduled for 6th of October 1982 and he was transferred to Luzerne County Prison. He was calm and collected for the first couple of days in the lockup but he quickly started threatening the guards and even told them that he would commit suicide in his cell. He was put on round the clock watch and the guards didn't let him out of their sight.

The defense called Dr. Anthony Turchetti who conducted various examinations in order to determine if George Banks was coherent and that he understood the charges. Dr. Turchetti told them that Banks was not insane and that he could go through the trial. Banks didn't want to be tried in his hometown of Wilkes-Barre but the judge denied his plea. Instead, he made sure that the jury was selected from Pittsburgh, Pennsylvania because they didn't know the people involved in the case.

The trial began on 6th of June 1983. The prosecution was confident knowing that they have plenty of evidence to prove that George Banks was not insane and that he was of clear mind on the day of the murders. They had more than forty witnesses who were ready to talk about Banks' behavior prior to the killings. The evidence also included crime scene photos and his rifle.

On the other hand, George Banks was completely against the insanity plea. He claimed that he was innocent and that the police shot some of his wounded victims. However, his own attorneys did prepare the defense that would rely on his fragile state of mind, as well as the unusual lifestyle he led. After all, he has several girlfriends living with him at the time and the settings did remind the authorities of a cult-like place.

The trial was opened with the statement from Dr. Spodak, a psychiatrist who told the jury about the mental state of George Banks. He said that Banks was paranoid and suicidal. Banks would often talk about being a victim of a conspiracy and that the entire township was against him. The prosecution asked Dr. Spodak about his evaluation of the accused and is it possible that George Banks was faking the insanity. Dr. Spodak told them that he was certain Banks did believe in everything he said and that he was clearly delusional.

George Banks wanted to take the stand and tell the court his side of the story. His attorneys were against this because it would appear that he was not mentally ill and that his testimony would endanger their whole case. However, stopping Banks was almost impossible.

Once he got to the stand, Banks started rambling without any clear timeline of the events. He would jump from one killing to another without providing enough information to the courtroom. His demeanor was also odd because he simply couldn't sit still. He then dove into the conspiracy claims, saying that the police was out to get him because he has a mixed background and once again repeated the story that the law enforcement killed the remaining members of his family who were still alive after he shot them.

The defense tried salvaging their case by inviting Banks' mother and advisor to the stand. They were supposed to confirm that Banks suffered from a mental illness. However, the jury was already in shock after George's testimony and appeared completely uninterested in anything they had to say. It was time for the prosecution's side of the story.

They called James Olsen, who was one of the survivors from Schoolhouse Lane murders. He fully recovered and was fit to testify. Olsen told the courtroom that George Banks was the man who shot him and drove away, leaving him to die in front of his home. The prosecution then called the detectives who arrived at the crime scene at Schoolhouse Lane and they described everything they saw inside

Banks' home. Their testimony had plenty of visuals because they also showed the crime scene photos.

The closing statements were delivered on 21st of June 1983. The defense attorneys once again repeated that Banks' mental health was questionable and that he was going through a lot of stress at the time when the murders were committed. They pointed out the custody battle and the loss of his job as a prison guard.

The prosecution pointed out Banks' criminal past and that he was prone to violence. They claimed that Banks knew exactly what he was doing on the day of the shootings and that he shouldn't have been out of the prison at all.

The judge talked to the jury for almost half an hour, giving them the last instructions before they exit the courtroom and start the deliberation. It didn't take them a long time to find George Banks guilty on all charges. Not a single member of the jury believed that Banks was insane or mentally unstable so they made their decision quickly.

The sentencing was delivered on 22nd of June. The jury returned to the courtroom after five and a half hours. The foreman stepped up and delivered the sentence. George Banks was found guilty on all charges and the jury recommended the death penalty. Banks stood calmly by his seat and his only comment was to the juror who was clearly distressed. He told her: "It's not your fault, ma'am. You were lied to. A two-hour exhumation would clear me."

George Banks was driven straight to Huntingdon maximum security prison after the sentencing. He stayed there until 1985. His attorneys were trying to overturn the conviction in front of the US Supreme Court but once their case was dismissed, Banks was transferred to State Correctional Institute at Graterford where he was locked up back in the 1960s.

The aftermath

George Banks continued his fight from the prison. His attorneys did their best to get him an appeal but the US Supreme Court turned it down every single time. The defense was set on proving that George Banks was mentally ill and that he shouldn't have been on trial in the first place. Banks have been placed on the list for execution twice since the imprisonment but the death penalty was delayed both times.

The reason behind the canceling of the executions was due to the fact that George Banks was indeed mentally ill. His paranoid schizophrenia took a toll on his mind and delivering the death penalty to someone who is not even aware of his surroundings simply doesn't feel right. Banks tried to commit suicide while incarcerated at least a couple of times so it is clear that he is not afraid to die.

Now, more than three decades after the murders, George Banks still stands behind his convictions that he murdered his children because he wanted to spare them the horrors of being mixed race. It appears that he really believed in the upcoming race wars. He continues to blame the law enforcement for shooting the children who survived the killing spree.

The residents of the Greater Wyoming Valley still remember that day in September of 1982 when the entire area was fearing the deranged shooter who was on the loose. It is one of the most well-known crimes in the area and a larger tragedy was prevented because the police reacted quickly. George Banks was very ill and he probably would have continued his killing spree, making this tragedy even bigger.

9 798224 944903